Intro

In late 1999 ... r charts together to c... for my students on th... es I ran in my home coun... carried away with the pr... booklet prepared and the project took on a life of its own. 'Nightscenes' 2000 was printed by my poor trusty home printer but, as a regular contributor on BBC Radio Lincolnshire, once the word got out that it was available, 200 copies later and the printer was ready to call a solicitor! Thus for subsequent editions it has been professionally printed by a local firm in Horncastle, Cupits, and a fine job they do as well. Needless to say Nightscenes continues to grow in popularity with retailers now stocking it Nationwide. So what's this thingy then - the 'Companion'?

Nightscenes was always intended for public consumption and within its pages are many references to all sorts of astronomical and space related terms and meanings. Thus it can be bewildering to the newcomer to the subject when things like conjunction, aphelion and the like, crop up. The yearly Nightscenes simply doesn't have room to give an adequate description - otherwise it would amount to a dictionary the size of a major reference book and cost far too much for an annual publication. Thus I felt the need for the 'Companion'. In simple terms it covers the basic astronomical/space terms that are likely to appear in the yearly 'Nightscenes' but the 'Companion' is not and never pretends to be a complete reference book on all things astronomical - again the subject matter is too vast and complicated. Thus 'Companion' is meant to be used in conjunction (good astronomical word that!) with the yearbook so that when reference is made to say, "Jupiter is in conjunction with the Sun on so and so date", you will know what it is referring to. I do hope that the 'Companion' and 'Nightscenes' are useful to all who are fascinated with the night sky and that the reader enjoys many clear skies whilst pursuing the delights of the Universe.

My thanks go to my family, my many astronomy friends across the country and abroad, my friends at BBC Radio Lincolnshire, the many Stockist's of Nightscenes across the country and Cupit Print for their continued support. Special thanks go to Lorraine, my wife, for her unstinting support and help in proof reading as this publication progressed and keeping pushing me in producing the book!

If you have Internet access & you find the Universe as fascinating as the author then why not take a look at the Astrospace web site:

www.astrospace.co.uk

There you will find links to NASA, ESA and other Space Agencies, Local & National Astronomical Societies and an online version published on a monthly basis of Nightscenes. The Internet version enables me to provide updates if a new event occurs such as a bright comet or Nova if they are visible. There is plenty to keep the interested sky watcher 'surfing' for hours! The author is available at times to give talks to a wide variety of groups including Schools, Societies, Clubs etc, so if you are interested and would like more information then write or e-mail me via the following:

To Annie Best wishes Paul Money

Paul L Money **FRAS FBIS**

18 College Park, Horncastle, Lincs, LN9 6RE

e-mail : talks@astrospace.co.uk

Good observing and many clear skies!

Understanding the monthly sky charts

When we browse through a guide to the night sky, often the charts are portrayed as 'all sky charts' usually for a particular time at either the start of a month or the middle of it. The first is the view adopted by Nightscenes and a typical chart with South at the bottom is shown below with a key to some of the more important things I will be dealing with in this book. But what does this chart actually mean and show us? Orange lines streaking away from a particular point on the chart show the region from where meteors may appear to radiate from. Where possible the weekly phase of the Moon is shown against the relevant constellation, if it lies on the chart. This usually means that only the 1st Quarter Moon and Full Moon can be shown in the timeframe of the chart shown. Planet positions are given for the middle of the month and their names are in green. Occasionally, on some charts, selected important Stars and Deep Sky Objects (usually referred to in the monthly text) are highlighted in light blue or red. The main Constellations are

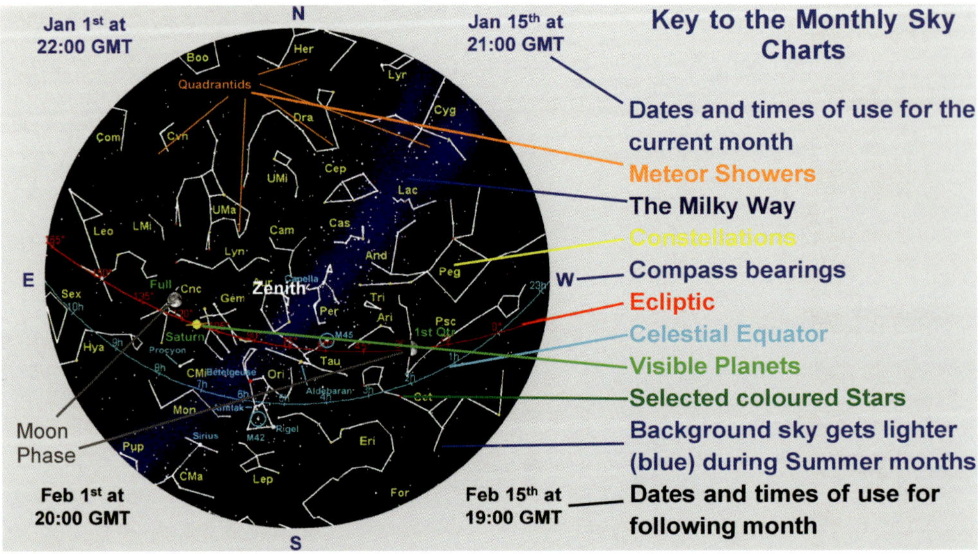

shown with stars as faint as about magnitude 5.5. Thus all the Constellations visible for the time and date of the chart are shown with most naked eye stars plotted. Note that under light polluted skies only the brighter stars and therefore constellations will be visible to the unaided eye. It is a sad legacy of our times that we throw away energy into the night sky unnecessarily and so spoil our night time natural heritage view of the heavens. The Nightscenes charts also try to show that during the Summer months the night sky is not particularly dark for those of us living in the Northern Hemisphere at the latitudes of the UK and Ireland. Thus the background colour of the sky changes from black in Winter months to a pale blue for the Summer months. In the Winter, the Milky Way (the disk of our Galaxy) can be seen quite clearly as a milky band (hence the name) running across the sky when seen from a nice dark site, but it fades as the night sky gets lighter as we progress into Summer.

The **Ecliptic** is the apparent path of the Earths orbit projected against the background stars and constellations. For us on the Earth it appears to be the path of the Sun as it moves through the constellations during the course of a year. The **Celestial Equator** is the projection of the Earths Equator into space - more on them later.

The outer edge of the chart represents the horizon. So take a look around you for 360 degrees. Your view of the distant horizon is actually a circle centred on you. Your feet are at the centre of the circle and therefore are on the ground, but the **SKY** is above you like a great dome and the outer edge of our chart is the place where that great dome appears to meet the ground at the horizon. The centre of the great dome lies directly ***above*** your head and this is the centre of our chart and is known as the **ZENITH (Z)**. On the edge of the horizon is marked the normal points of the compass: **North (N)**, **South (S)**, **East (E)** and **West (W)**. Hang on, they're the wrong way round! When you look North then normally East is always on your right as seen in the chart on page 5! Think about this for a moment, then realise that ***you look DOWN*** at the chart but ***you*** *look UP* at the sky! So in reality you should actually hold the chart above your head - but that's a bit impractical. Try this for an experiment: Face North and look down. East is to your right, West is too your left and South is at the back. Now lie on the floor looking up with your head to the North and your feet towards the South. East is now on your ***left*** with West now on the ***right*** because you are looking 180° to your original view! Note that North and South remain the same. Incidentally North is 0°, East is 90°, South is 180° and West is therefore 270° around the horizon and measuring around your horizon in either degrees or with the compass is called the **AZIMUTH (Azm)**. Sometimes an object is measured upwards from the horizon in degrees and this is the **ALTITUDE (Alt)** of the object. Thus a planet, the moon or a star is said to be at an **Alt** of *x* number of degrees. The Zenith is naturally 90° from the horizon and you can't have an Alt of more than that!

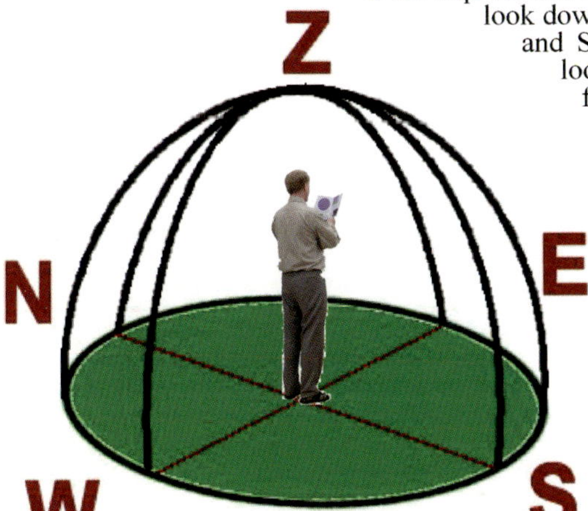

Looking East

So lets look again at the main chart on page 4 and see what it is telling us. Firstly note the date and time in each corner. The top two are highlighted in blue and indicate the dates in the *current* month when that chart represents the sky. However, notice that over the course of two weeks, the same sky can be seen an hour earlier. The bottom two dates carry this idea over into the next month and is shown in black so you can see that although the chart is set for Jan 1st at 22:00 GMT (10pm) it also shows the same sky on Feb 1st at 20:00 GMT (8pm) . You can use this to also work out other dates when that particular chart can be used when the sky is dark enough. But when the times move into times of daylight then naturally you can't see the stars! Thus although you can work out that the same sky can be seen at 16:00 GMT (4pm) on April 1st (lets not worry about BST for the moment!) that time is actually during daylight so the light from the Sun drowns out the stars and constellations and we can't see them. They are still there but the sky is simply too bright to view them.

Now for the four main compass points which are shown around the horizon. Let's say you want to look towards the East on February 1st at 20:00 GMT (8pm). You hold the appropriate chart and rotate it until the horizon you are facing is at the bottom of the chart as shown in the example here (ignore the fact that the writing is the wrong way round - that's irrelevant to the sky itself!). So East is now in front of you matching the fact you are facing East. The middle of the chart is still above you and now West is the area of sky behind you with South on your right and North on your left. So whichever horizon you are looking at for real, just rotate the chart until that horizon is at the bottom and therefore in front of you.

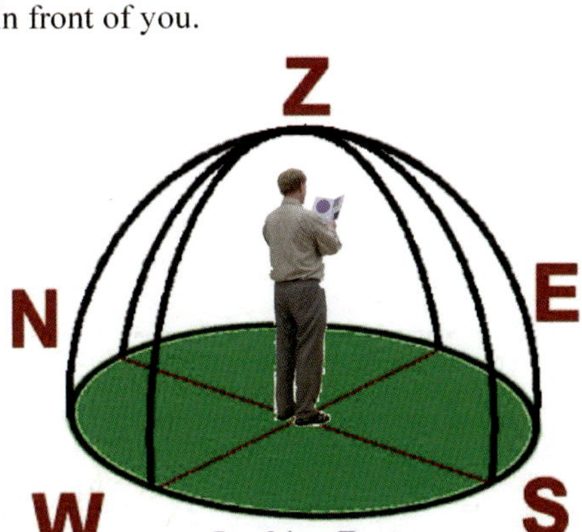

Looking East

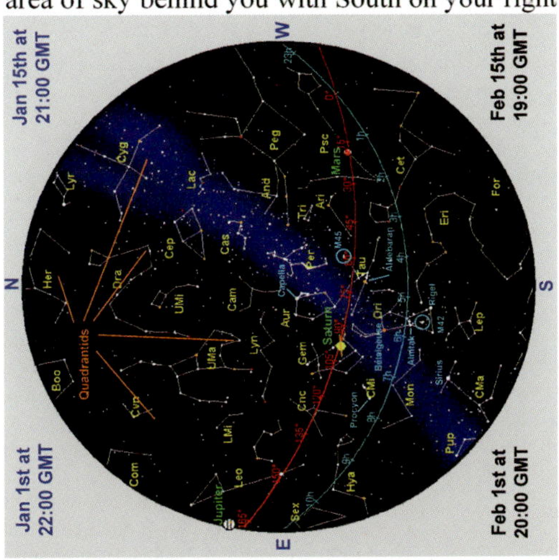

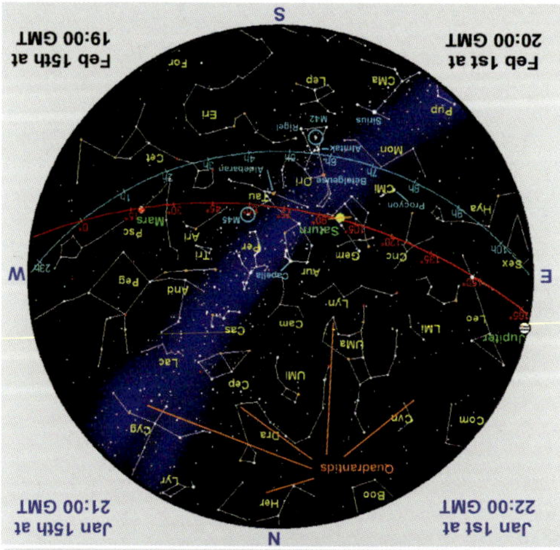

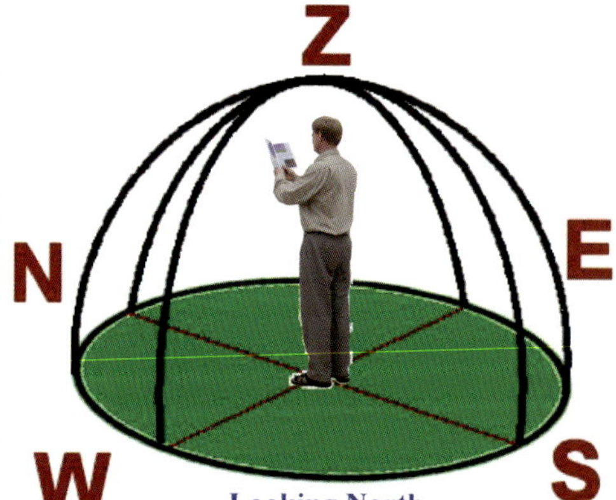

Looking North

Look North and hold the chart with North at the bottom as the charts above show. Look West and put West at the bottom as the next charts indicate and so on and so forth. The centre of the chart will ***ALWAYS*** be directly above your head (so don't strain your neck!!).

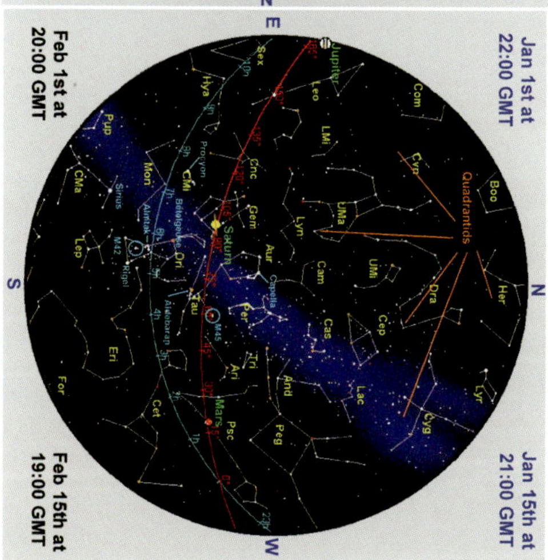

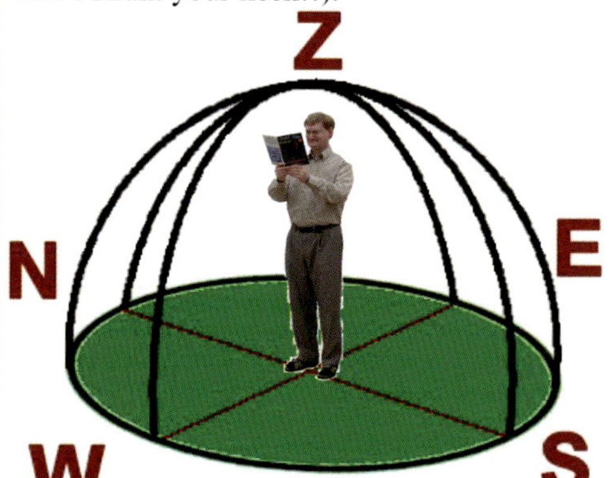

Looking West

If you are not sure of your compass bearings then one trick is to note where the Sun is at midday - by then it should be over in the South. Remember to take into account British Summer Time* if it is in force when you do this - so you may have to wait another hour to allow the Sun to reach the proper place in the sky. Then if you stand with your back to the Sun you will be facing North. East will be to your right and therefore West will be to your left. Note any features that lie in the same direction as those compass points (neighbour's house, a particular tree or telegraph pole, etc.) and you should be able to find your direction at any time of day or night.

* (also known as Daylight Saving Time or Summer Time).

I've already noted that you can use the charts on other dates and times - but why is this so? It comes down to the plain fact that we live on a moving platform and that one of the motions we experience is the Earth orbiting the Sun, taking 1 year (i.e. 12 months) to do so. Thus with each passing month our viewpoint of the heavens changes making it look like the sky appearing to slowly rotate completely round us. With each passing day the Stars rise 3 minutes and 56 seconds earlier, multiply that by 14 days gives a difference of 55 minutes - nearly 1 hour. So this is why the charts can be used approximately an hour earlier with the passage of every two weeks, or about two hours earlier per month.

But there is a second motion of the Earth that we always seem to take for granted. The Earth spins about its axis of rotation and does so, with respect to the Sun, in 24 hours. So from our point of view on the Earths' surface it looks as though the whole sky rotates about the Earth in 24 hours. Think of it like this: instead of the charts representing the change in a month, now think of it in terms of the rotation of the Earth by 2 hours for each chart. So 2 multiplied by 12 charts gives, you've guessed it, 24 hours i.e. a full rotation of our planet about its axis. So if the January chart represents 10pm on Jan 1st then the February 1st chart = midnight, March 1st becomes 2am and so on as shown below. The example conveniently uses January 1st as its starting point at 10pm and, with the passing hours, the sky rotates from East to West (with the North polar

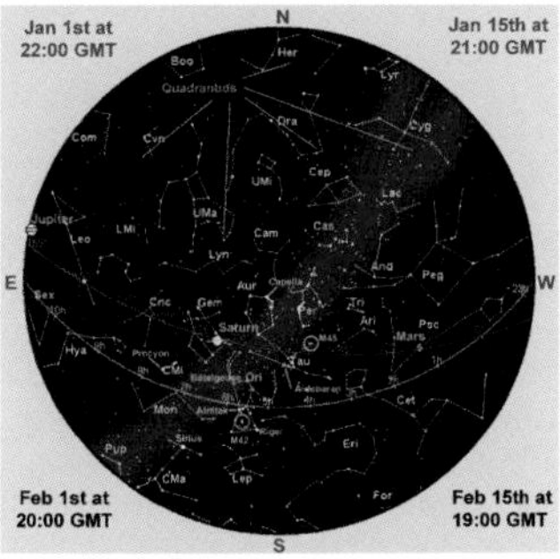

10pm (January 1st)

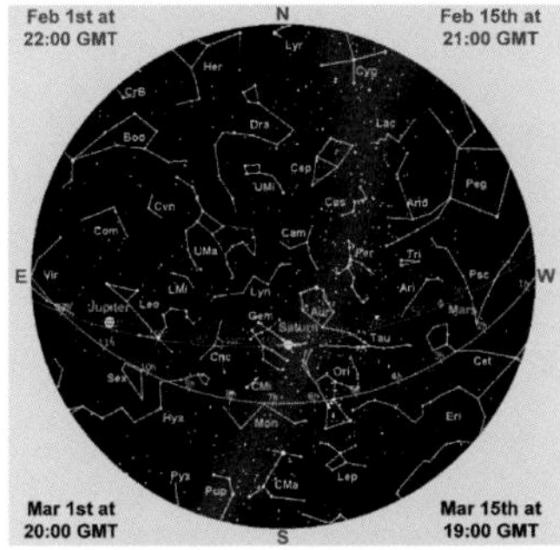

Midnight (January 2nd)

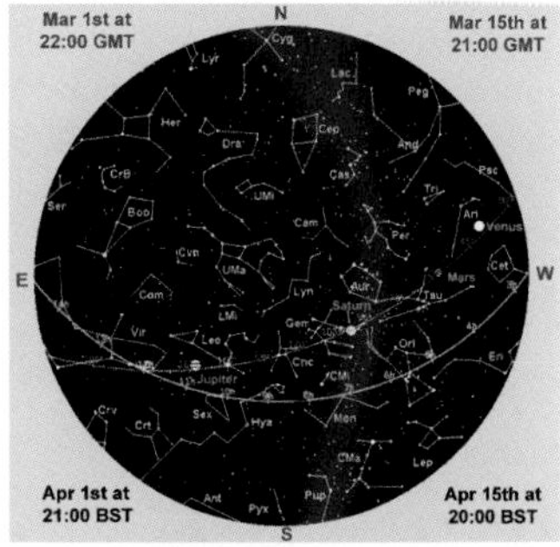

2am (January 2nd)

axis seemingly fixed at the North Pole Star, Polaris. You can use any of the charts to start with instead of just January. In the example below we shall use the September 1st chart at 11pm (BST) however, now the August chart represents the sky 2 hours earlier i.e. for 9pm BST Sept 1st and

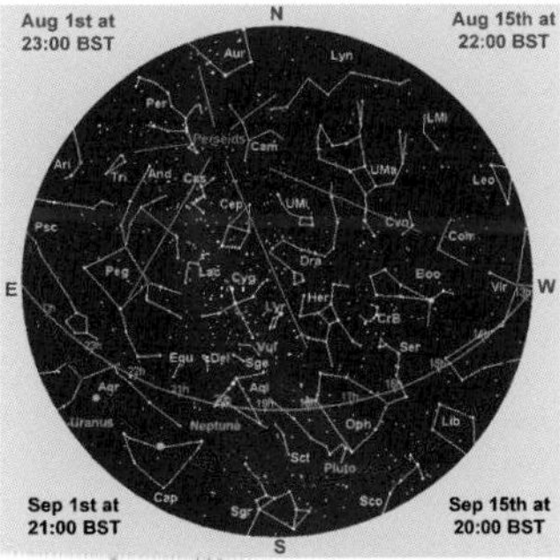

9pm (September 1st)

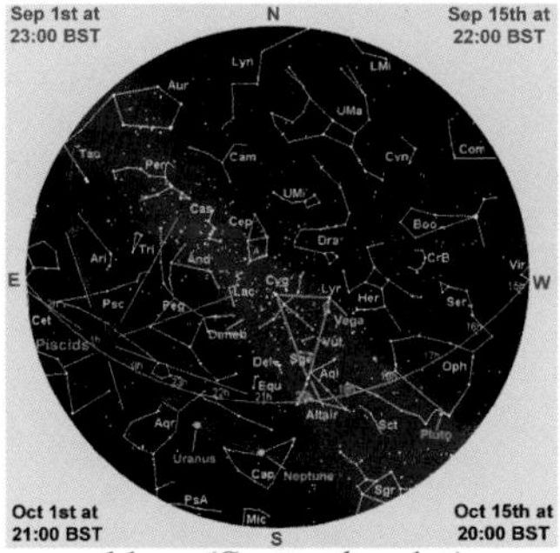

11pm (September 1st)

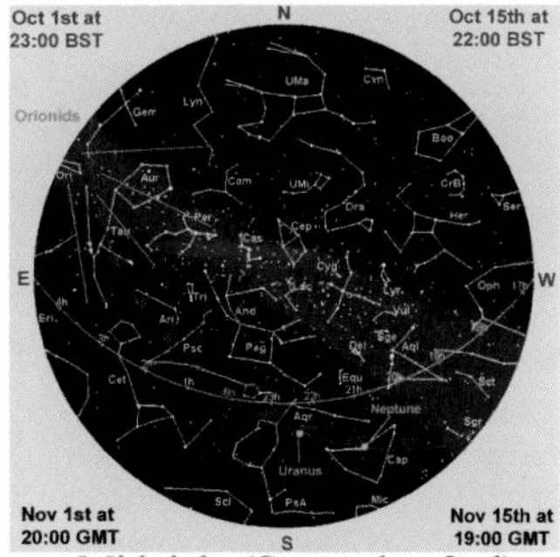

Midnight (September 2nd)

the October chart becomes Midnight for September 2nd. Thus any of the charts can act as your starting point for observing the motion of the sky during one evening. However, in the above case, because you are using the 'August chart' to represent 9pm for a month later - the sky will now be dark instead of the lighter background sky of the Summer month. Note also that any Meteor 'streaks' on the charts are only for the original date of the chart and so the Meteors will not be seen from those positions on different nights and months.

You should be able to estimate which charts to use depending upon your starting time as well so really the charts are even more useful when you know how! From page 15 the 12 monthly charts are reproduced at the lower right of each odd numbered page and you can flip through the pages to watch the night sky change both on daily basis and during a full year as well. These charts are set for 2004 and show how the planets were seen at different times of the year and of course during the course of a night so for example Saturn started 2004 near the centre of the chart with Jupiter just poking over the eastern horizon. By April Saturn was lower in the western sky whilst Jupiter lay due south and well placed to view. In June Saturn was no longer visible for the time of the chart with Jupiter getting lower towards the WSW. September and October saw the far outer giants of Uranus and Neptune in the south with no other bright planets visible. Finally by December we had lost Neptune but Uranus was still shown and Saturn had returned to the eastern sky.

Look carefully at Saturn's position for January and compare it with December. It began 2004 near the feet of Gemini (the Twins) but ended the year almost level with Gemini's two brightest stars (Castor and Pollux). This shows how much even Saturn moved along its orbit during just one earth year. The distant planets like Uranus, Neptune and faint Pluto, move a very small amount along their orbit in a year whilst mighty Jupiter moves through the equivalent of a full constellation. The innermost planets of Mercury and Venus both act as the 'Morning' and 'Evening' stars and Mars is at its best every two years. I shall look at their motion against the background stars a little later in this book. Meanwhile as you flip through the pages watching the monthly charts change, keep an eye on the Milky Way as it seems to drift across the sky and you will get an idea of when it's best to see it arching overhead. I personally find that the best views I have had from the UK of the Summer Milky Way is either in the early hours of the morning during February and March and from September to October in the early evening sky.

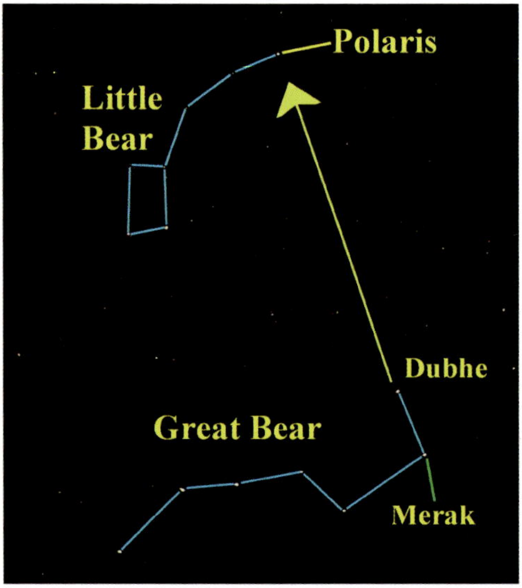

Of Tilts, Seasons and the Celestial Sphere

The **Celestial Sphere** is the complete sky (i.e. the Universe!) appearing to be wrapped around the Earth. Naturally we can only see half the sky at any one time from the surface but if you was lucky enough to go into space and far enough so that the Earth was quite small, then the entire sky would appear to be wrapped around you instead. From our Northern Hemisphere position on the Earth, our half of the sky appears to rotate around an average but naked eye star called Polaris - the (North) Pole Star. To find it, locate the constellation of the Great Bear or Ursa Major to give it its Latin name. The brightest seven stars form an asterism (group of stars) called the **Plough** or the **Saucepan,** these stars are usually the ones most people can find. The two right hand stars of the bowl of the saucepan are called Dubhe & Merak, known together as the 'Pointers' as they point towards Polaris and this is shown at left.

Of course if you are looking at the Pole Star then it follows that you are also looking North! Your right side points towards East, your left side West, therefore South must be behind you. Thus it's easy to work out which way you are looking or which way to look for an event! The height or altitude above the North horizon of the Pole Star depends on your position on the Earth's surface. Thus for my latitude of 53°12' N the Pole Star lies 53°12' above the North Horizon. If I lived at the Equator then my latitude would be 0° and so Polaris would be 0° above the horizon - on the horizon itself. So you can take it from there that whatever your latitude on the Earth is (in the Northern Hemisphere) then the North Pole Star, Polaris, will be that altitude above the North horizon. Of course this also means that if you are at the North Pole then Polaris is directly above you at an altitude of 90° and you will be very cold indeed! The altitude of the Pole Star is just a reflection of anyone's particular position on the Earths surface in the Northern Hemisphere. In the Southern Hemisphere they are not lucky enough to have a reasonably bright star close to their South Polar point. Strictly speaking Polaris itself is not exactly at the polar point but is about ½° away from it but visually it's close enough for most basic purposes.

The rotation of the stars about the North Polar Axis - close to Polaris

Depending on your latitude some of the Constellations such as Ursa Major (the Great Bear) and Cassiopeia will always be above the horizon and these are referred to as being Circumpolar. Most of the other Constellations rise & set during the course of the night and also vary in how well they are seen during the course of the year. Thus Orion dominates the Winter & Spring skies but is not visible during the Summer when it is only above the horizon during daylight hours and thus not observable. At right we see a picture of the Pole Star and Ursa Minor (the Little Bear). All the stars on that picture are Circumpolar but now look at the picture on the next page. At its

top is Cassiopeia and at centre lies Perseus. Cassiopeia is fully circumpolar along with the majority of Perseus. The bright star Capella lies at lower left and is just Circumpolar for my latitude but the orange and blue star trails at lower right (part of Aries) rise and set during the course of each 24 hour day. Note that all the stars rotate about the North Pole anti-clockwise.

The next illustration shows which stars rise and set, which are circumpolar and the relation between the angle of the pole star and the angle of a star on the Celestial Equator.

First, angle 'a' represents the angle or altitude of the Pole Star, Polaris, which naturally lies towards the North. Stars 1, 2 and 3 are circumpolar and so never set - always being above the horizon whether it be day or night. Star 4 only just dips below the horizon so sets for just a short while. Stars 5,6 and 7 spend a greater and greater amount of their time below the horizon rising in the east and setting in the west. They reach their greatest height above the Southern horizon half way between the two. In the case of star 7, it lies on the Celestial Equator and is 90° from Polaris. Thus it rises due East and sets due West all the time. From the illustration it can be seen that there is a simple relationship between the altitude of the Pole Star and the angle star 7 (and therefore the Celestial Equator) makes with a vertical axis - they are both the same! So if Polaris is at

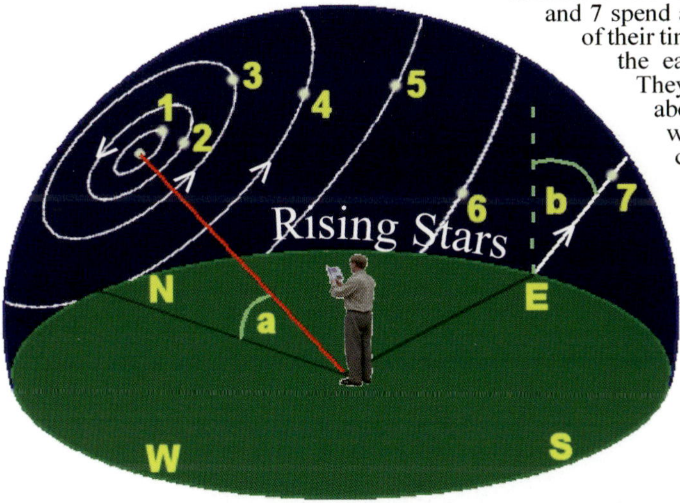

30° then star 7 rises at an angle of 30° from the vertical as well. Now look at the illustration here at right. This time we are looking due South. Star 7 still lies on the Celestial Equator but as you look towards the Southern Horizon stars 8,9 and 10 spend less and less time above the horizon as you are trying to look towards the South Celestial Pole - which naturally lies below the horizon for those of us in the Northern Hemisphere. Star 10 barely gets above the horizon and so would not be an easy object to view - especially if there is a lot of haze or you have buildings, trees and the general landscape in the way. All Stars rise in the East and set in the West regardless of where you are in the

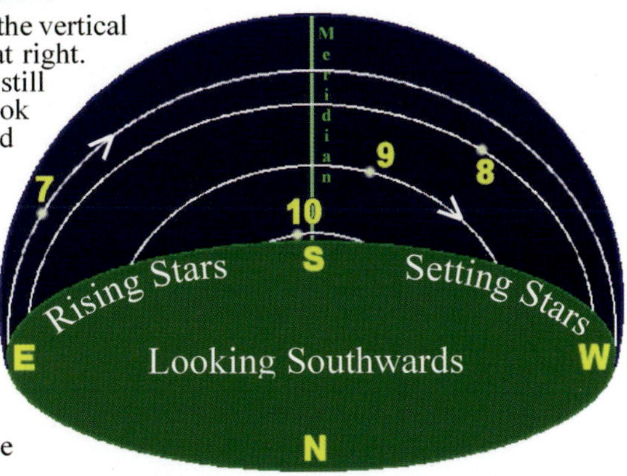

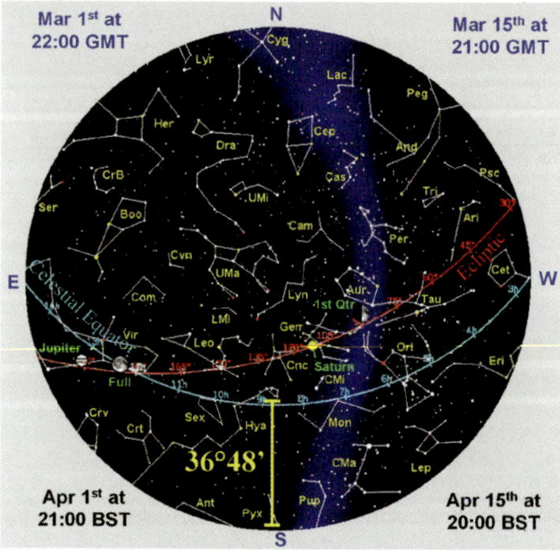

world and hopefully the two illustrations on the previous page shows why some stars are easier to view than others.

On the Monthly charts there are two curved lines on the Celestial Sphere that intersect each other. These lines are the **Celestial Equator (CE) (shown in blue)** & the **Ecliptic (Ec) (in red)**. Imagine the Earth's ***Equator*** extended out into space. Where it meets the **Celestial Sphere** it cuts this sphere in half and the line marking this is the **Celestial Equator**. By checking through all the charts you will see it never changes position, always beginning in the East & finishing in the West and reaching its greatest height (or Altitude) above the horizon due South. This height in degrees can be found by the simple relation of 90° minus your Latitude on the Earth so for example the Charts are set for Horncastle in Lincolnshire which is at 53°12' N which taken from 90° gives a height of 36°48' for the Celestial Equator as it crosses the sky due South. From somewhere like the Algarve in southern Portugal the latitude is approx 37° so the Celestial Equator would then be 53° above the southern horizon. This also explains why if you travel south round the Earths surface then you see more of the southern area of the sky but at the price of losing the equivalent number of degrees of sky in the north.

Meanwhile the **Ecliptic** is the path the Sun appears to take amongst the background stars. This time imagine the Earths ***Orbit*** around the Sun extended into space as a flat plane. Where this plane intersects the sky it too cuts the sky in half and this line is the **Ecliptic**. From our point of view the Sun appears to orbit the Earth and so the Sun follows the Ecliptic, journeying along it during the course of 1 year. Because the Earth is tilted with respect to its orbit by 23° 26' this gives rise to two intersection points where the Ecliptic and Celestial Equator meet called the **Equinox's**. This tilt of the Earth also gives us our ***Seasons***. If there was no tilt then the Ecliptic would be the same as the Celestial Equator (and life would be boring with no seasons!). The intersection point that lies in the Constellation of Pisces (Psc) is the **Vernal (Spring) Equinox** otherwise known as the First Point of Aries (note Precession has carried it into Pisces since it was first named several thousand years ago!). The Sun reaches this point on the 20th or 21st March. The second is the **Autumnal Equinox** which currently lies in Virgo (Vir) and is reached on 22nd or 23rd September. Leap years account for the different dates.

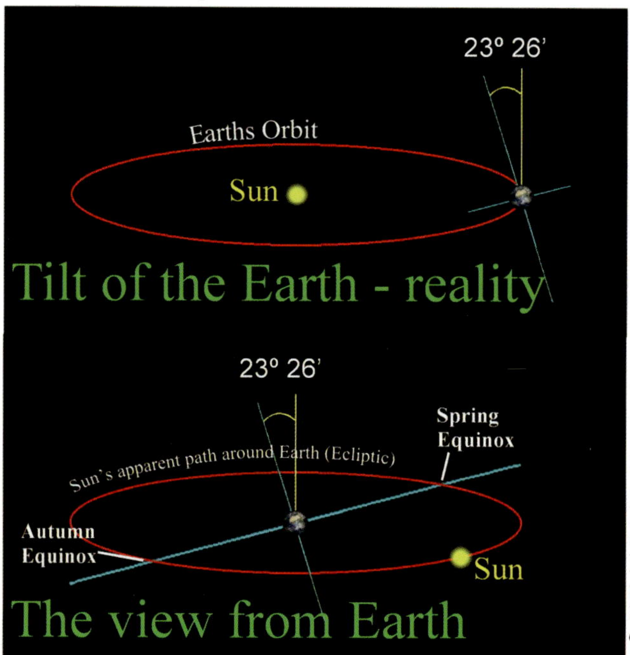

Because the Ecliptic is inclined to the Celestial Equator it follows that it can, at times, be higher in the sky than the Celestial Equator and at other times it can lie below it. Thus at its highest (for Horncastle) the Ecliptic can be 36°48' + 23°26' = 60°14' above the southern horizon. When

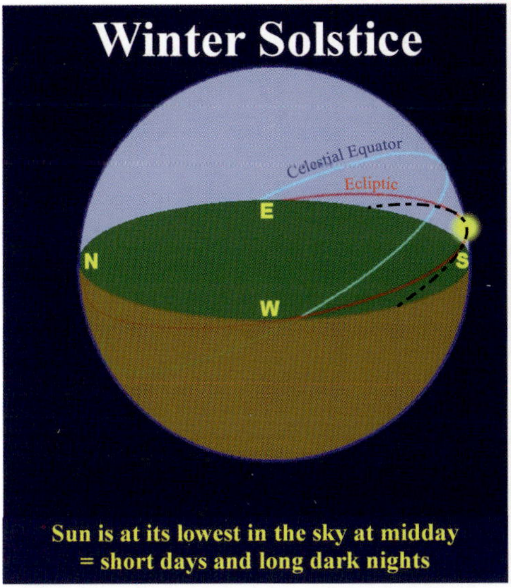

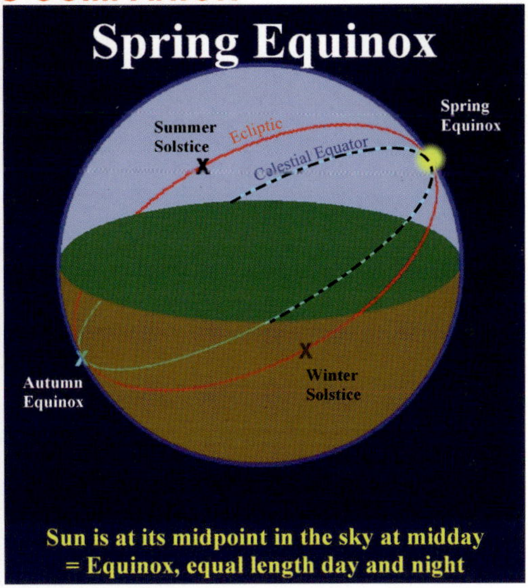

the Sun reaches this point it is the **Summer Solstice** and is 90° Eastwards from the Vernal Equinox lying just inside the Constellation of Taurus on the border with Gemini & Orion. At its lowest the answer is 36°48' - 23°26' = 13°12' above the horizon and this point is the **Winter Solstice**, lying 270° Eastwards from the Vernal Equinox and is in Sagittarius - which is why it always appears low from the UK and Ireland when it lies in the south and so the Sun is always low in the sky during Winter. The situation is reversed for those in the Southern Hemisphere. The illustrations on this page help to show how much the Sun's altitude varies during the seasons. During Winter the Sun travels a path that is below the Celestial Equator and so it never gets very high in the sky for mid northern latitudes. It rises in the SE and sets in the SW. At the Spring and Autumn Equinox's the Sun lies **on** the Celestial Equator at the point where the Ecliptic crosses it and so the Sun rises due East and sets due West giving us twelve hours of day and night. By the Summer Solstice the Sun now lies above the Celestial Equator and spends a long time above the daytime horizon. It rises in the NE and takes approx 18 hours before setting in the NW giving us our long hours of daylight and a short twilight night. The bottom illustration combines the above three for someone who lies closer to the equator. It's important to realise that the ecliptic line does not

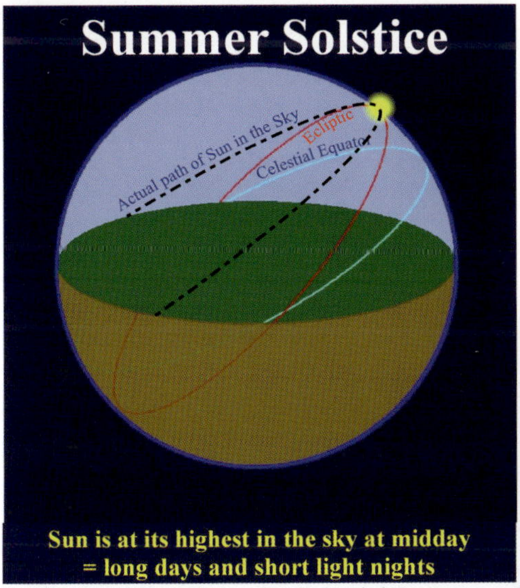

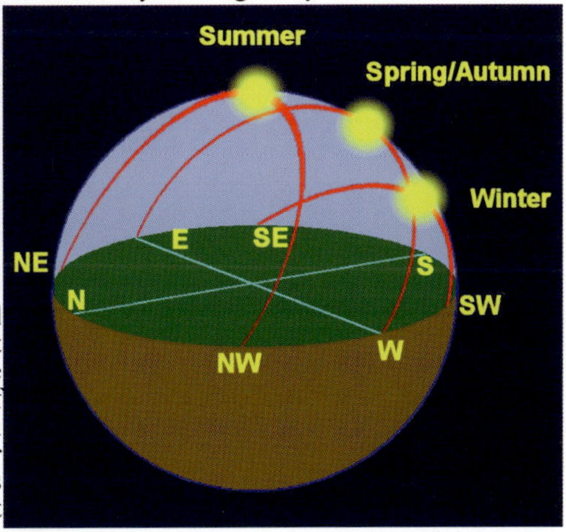

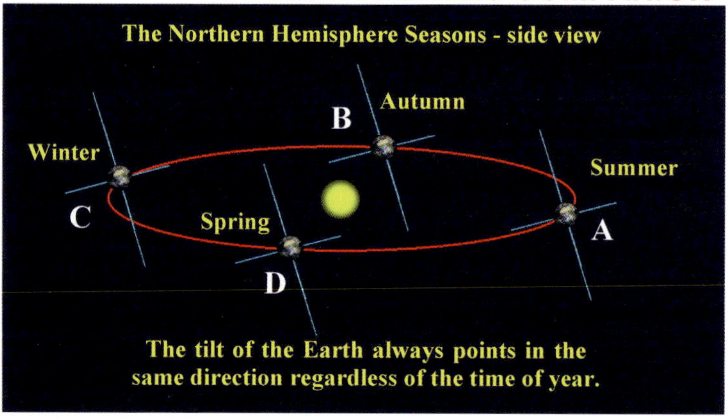

represent the actual path of the Sun across the sky during a single day but represents the path of the Sun during one year. Hence the black dashed lines on the previous charts show the real daily path of the Sun across the sky.

Now lets look at the other effect of the seasons - how they change which constellations are seen during the year. The tilt of the Earth gives us our seasons and combined with the position of the Sun along the Ecliptic alters what we can see subtly with each passing night. Over the month's this has a dramatic effect on the constellations that are easily visible. The lower illustration combined with the one above enables us to understand why Orion cannot be seen at night in the Summer whilst the Autumn constellations cannot be seen during the Spring etc.

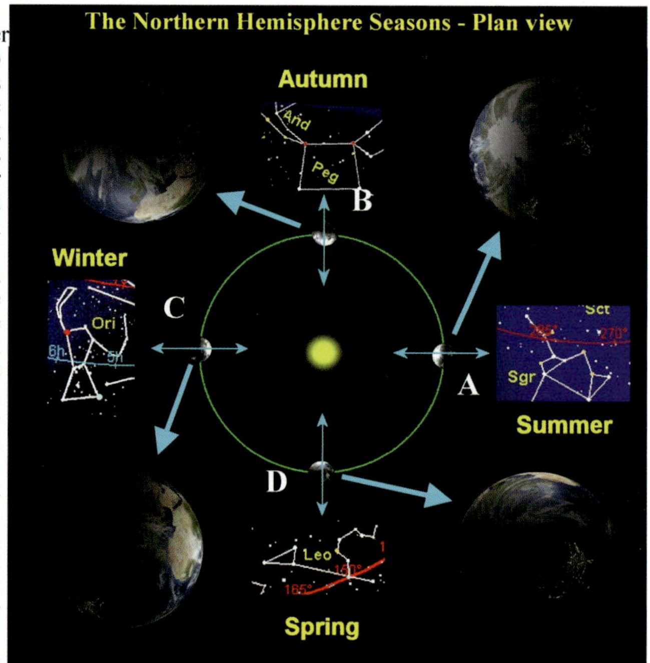

At 'A' it is Summer (for the Northern Hemisphere) and the Summer constellations of Sagittarius and Scorpius etc are visible at night but during the day we see that the Sun lies in the direction of the Winter constellations such as Orion and Taurus thus they cannot be seen in the glare of daylight. At 'B' the direction opposite the Sun (i.e. night) shows that the Autumn constellations are visible at night (Pegasus and Andromeda, Pisces and Aries etc.) but during the Day the Sun lies amongst the stars of the Spring sky - such as Leo and Virgo.

At 'C' the Earth is at the opposite side of its orbit to 'A' and it is now Winter so Orion and Taurus are visible at night but now the Sun lies in the direction of the Summer constellations of Sagittarius etc. So they are the ones not visible at night. Finally at 'D' the night sky has the Spring constellations visible (Leo etc) whilst the Sun lies amongst the stars of Autumn and so those constellations are not visible.

Now combine the tilt of the Earth with your position on the Earths surface and things get more interesting. If you live at the North Pole - you'll be cold! However at both 'B' and 'D' you will experience 12 hours of day and night. But at 'A' you'll have 24 hours of daylight (for several months) - not good if you like viewing the night sky! Conversely at 'C' you will have 24 hours of Night - again for several months so I guess you'd be tired from too much observing! At the latitude of the British Isles the effect is less extreme but during the Summer we do still get quite light nights as the Sun doesn't get very far below our Northern horizon. The good news is that for most of the year the night skies are dark - except for the plague of Light Pollution in some areas.

Viewing the Inner Planets

Now lets turn our attention to the **Planets**. Planet means '***Wandering Star***' and so our ancient ancestors coined this term when they realised that not all the stars are fixed in the sky. We shall deal first with the two planets, Mercury and Venus and they are known as '**Inferior Planets**'. Lying inside our Earths orbit they spend a lot of time near the glare of the Sun. Thus viewing them can have its difficulties depending on not just where they are in their own orbits but also where the Earth lies along its orbit too. If we could view an inferior planets' orbit from above we should get a view like that at left. I have ignored the fact that their orbits are not

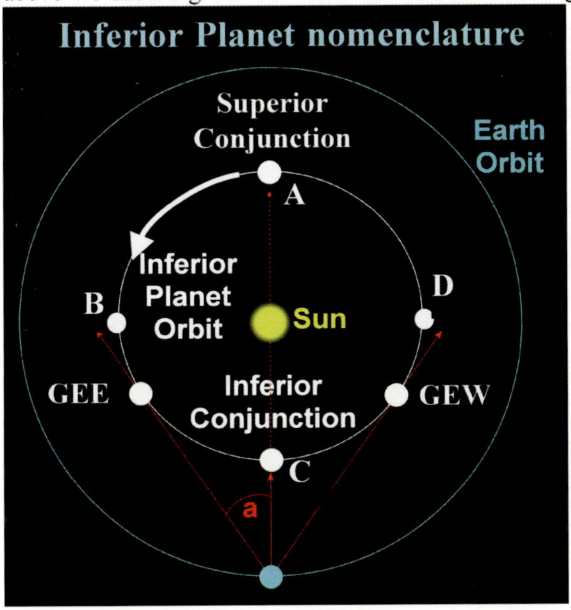

perfectly circular as that comes into play later in our examination. When an inferior planet lies on the far side of its orbit to the Earth and is in line with the Sun it is then at 'Superior Conjunction' and as a rule (but by no means always) it cannot be seen. As the planet moves round its orbit it slowly appears to the left of the Sun from the Earths (and observers) viewpoint and so it appears in the **Evening sky.** Now you would think that when it reaches point 'A' in its orbit it would be at its best to view but remember we're looking from ABOVE the solar system. In reality we are looking from the Earth in an orbit further out so it's when the planet reaches GEE that the planet appears furthest from the Sun in our sky. GEE means Greatest Elongation East as the planet lies to the East of the Sun and so lies in our evening sky. How good a view we have though is dependant upon the time of year the planet reaches GEE - more on that shortly. After GEE the planet appears to us to gradually move back in towards the glare of the Sun as it heads towards 'C' on our diagram. At 'C' it is at Inferior Conjunction and now lies between us and the Sun. The planet is also at its closest to us as well so this helps to make it larger in our telescopes and in the lead up to Inferior Conjunction it also helps to make it reasonably bright. At inferior conjunction, the vast majority occur when the planets orbital tilt to Earths takes it either above or below the disk of the Sun. However, at rare times, the planet can cross the disk of the Sun producing a **Transit**. A transit of Mercury occurred for the British Isles on May 7th 2003 and a much rarer transit of Venus occurred for us on June 8th 2004 as shown below. From 'C' the planet moves into the morning sky gradually getting further from the glare of the sun until it reaches GEW (Greatest Elongation West). At this point it is visible over in the eastern morning sky depending upon the time of year. After this the planets disk begins to shrink as it gets further away from the Earth and moves towards Superior Conjunction on the far side of the Sun when once again it will be difficult if not impossible to see. All of this occurs with an

Right: Mercury (small round dot upper centre) and a Sunspot (lower right) on May 7th 2003. Far Right: Venus nearing the end of its transit across the solar disk on June 8th 2004.

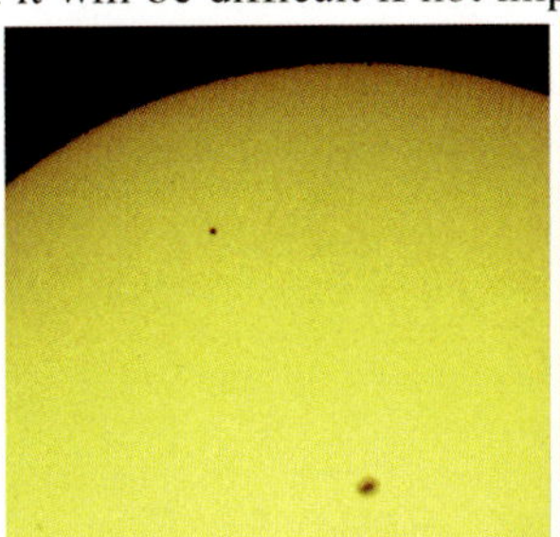

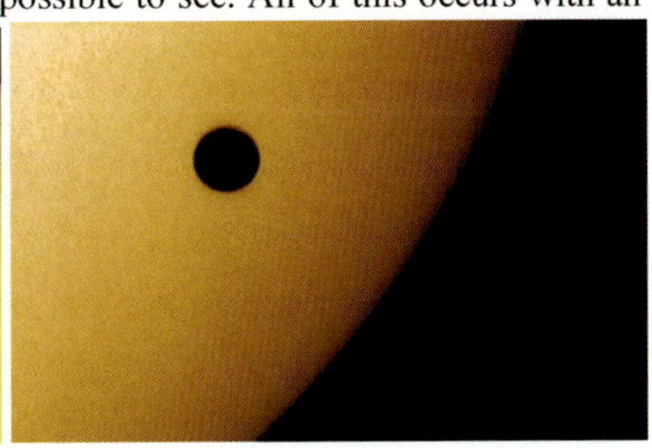

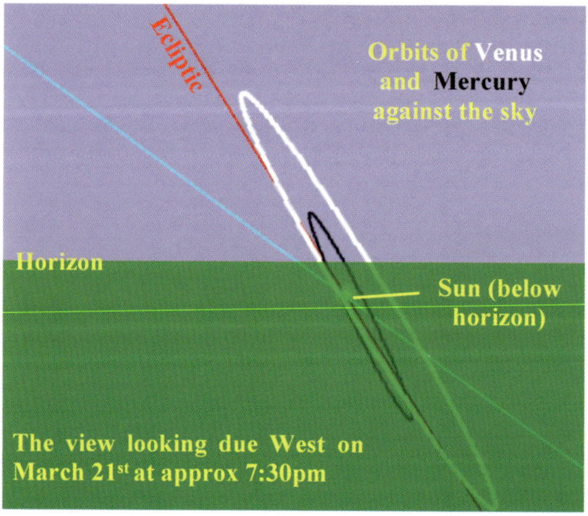

additional complicating factor - we live on a moving platform so the motion of the Earth itself affects how good a view we get and how long we wait until the planet is at its best to see.

Now lets look at the view we have of the above - but this time from the surface of the Earth and in particular our view from the Northern Hemisphere. This diagram at left shows the evening twilight sky for the Spring Equinox looking due West. Imaging that you can actually see the orbits of both inner planets superimposed on the background twilight sky. Note how steep the Ecliptic is compared with the horizon. It is this steep angle that lets us view both Mercury and Venus really well when they are in the right positions along their respective orbits. At this time of year the Ecliptic lies above the Celestial Equator and boosts our chances of viewing Mercury in particular. Mercury still lies in a bright twilight sky but at least we get about an hour or so to view it before it follows the sun below the horizon. Venus has a larger orbit and so when well placed it can be seen for several hours after sunset - indeed it gets far enough from the solar glare to be seen against a dark starlit sky. Six months later (right) the view is completely different. Now the ecliptic lies below the Celestial Equator and is at a very shallow angle to the horizon. Any planet lying along the ecliptic quickly sets soon after the Sun and is lost to view. Thus both Mercury and Venus may lie at their greatest elongation east but due to the time of year and poor angle of the ecliptic they will either be impossible or at best difficult to see.

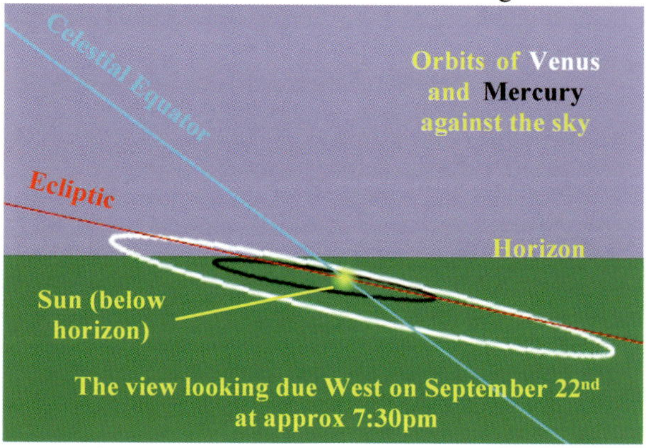

Interestingly the morning sky apparitions are the opposite to the above. The Spring Morning sky to the East (lower left chart) has a shallow ecliptic angle whilst the best morning apparitions take place in the Autumn (lower right chart) when the ecliptic is at its steepest. As a general rule then, the best time to view Mercury in the evening is late February to early April whilst the best time to view it in the morning sky is late August to early November. Because Venus gets so far from the Sun it has a much longer viewing period than its inner neighbour.

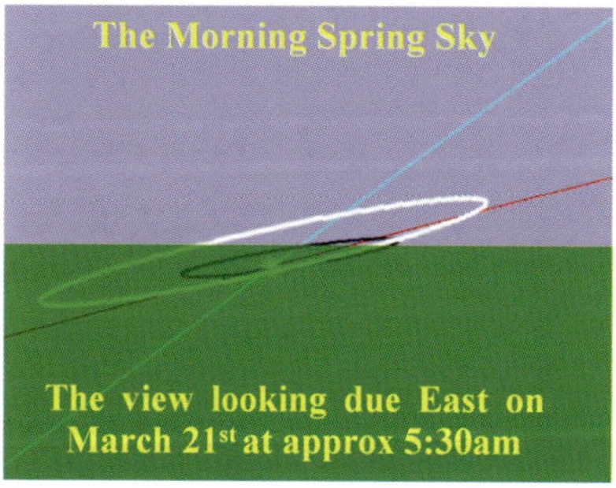

Mercury can be viewable at its best for up to 3 weeks compared with Venus which can often be seen for several months! The view on the next page shows both planets together in the dawn sky and is a favourite image of mine. Mercury is

(naturally) the fainter one over on the left. The diagram below shows the apparition of Mercury for

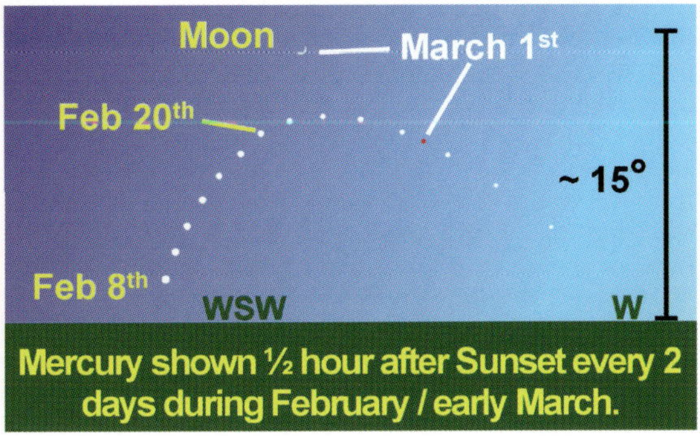

February/early March 2006 but the arc Mercury takes against the sky is not the same as its orbit as shown in the previous diagrams - so why is that?

It's all down to the fact that as Mercury moves along its orbit, it and the sky position it occupies on a daily basis is also moving because we live on a moving platform - the Earth. If our planet stayed still in space - not rotating nor moving along its orbit, then Mercury would follow the path as shown in the black orbit (below left) and it would first move up to the left then drop back down to the right as indicated by the black arrows. Instead the steady slipping of the sky

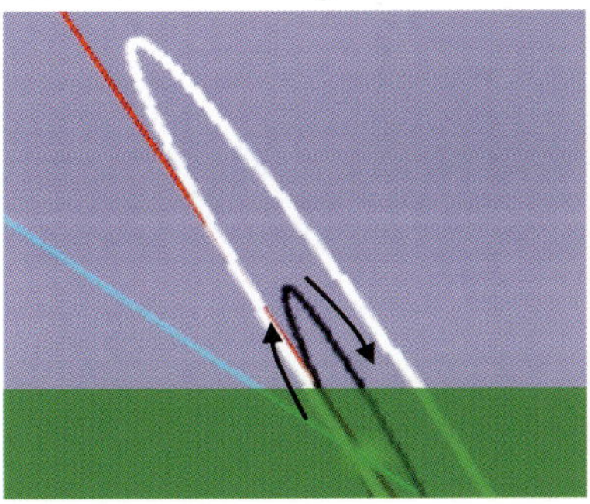

westwards as the Earth moves along its orbit means that Mercury's apparent position in the sky slips westward as well. Initially the inner planet has the advantage as it is moving rapidly upwards so it gains in height but slips only a little to the west . You can see this in the diagram above. From Feb 8th to the 24th its motion along its orbit should take it to the left and up but it nearly overcomes the westward slippage giving it a steeper rise into the evening sky. After it has reached Greatest Elongation East it starts to move westward and down along its orbit so this now adds to the westward slippage of the sky so it drops quickly down to the horizon and is lost to view. This also happens to Venus but as Venus spends longer above the horizon it takes a more leisurely pace as it moves up its orbit, but once past GEE it too seems to quickly head back towards the solar glare. Finally, if you have a telescope, both planets disks will show phases like the Moon. Venus' phases are shown here captured by the author during 2004 along with a single image of Mercury at almost half phase on June 28th 2005 (below). At its closest to us the crescent of Venus may be spotted with a humble pair of 10X50 Binoculars as it heads back towards the solar glare - but you have to be very careful not to view the Sun instead as that can seriously damage your eyes.

Venus and Mercury through a Telescope

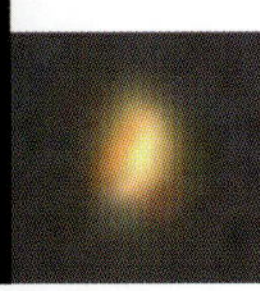

January Night Sky

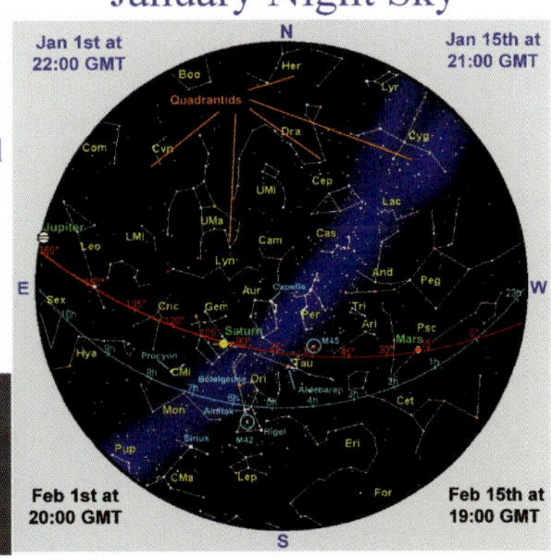

The Visibility of the Outer Planets

During the course of a year the Earths motion around the Sun along its orbit affects how well or otherwise we see the other planets and indeed the asteroids when those objects lie further from the Sun than the Earth. To us it appears that the Sun moves around us instead of the other way round. This means that, as we discussed several pages back, the visibility of the constellations depends upon the season and position of the Sun along the Ecliptic and that applies to the planets as well. The diagram here is a hypothetical example of the distribution of the planets along the ecliptic with the Sun's position marked for 3 places during the year. At 'A' The line from the Sun to the Earth and past it marks the boundary to what lies in the Evening sky and the Morning sky. The evening planets are to the left of this line and the morning planets are on the right of that line. At 'A' then, Saturn, Jupiter and Pluto all lie in the evening sky whilst Mars, Uranus and Neptune are in the morning sky. Mars is probably a bit close to the glare of the Sun to be easily seen in the morning twilight and Saturn will be in the early evening twilight sky. But

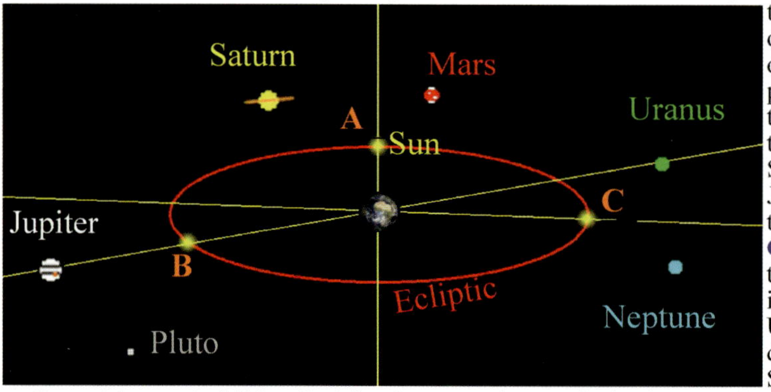

the rest are well spread out and so are observable. Now take position 'B' and note the line passing through Jupiter, the Sun, Earth and Uranus. Jupiter is in line with the Sun and so is at **Conjunction** and, with the much fainter Pluto, is not observable. Uranus, however, is directly opposite the Sun in our sky and so is at **Opposition** and visible all night. Saturn and Mars lie in the Morning half of the sky whilst Neptune is just past opposition and visible in the late evening. By 'C' both Neptune and Uranus are lost in the solar glare, Mars and Saturn are well placed to view in the evening sky. Jupiter is only a month or so from Opposition and with Pluto is visible for a large part of the night.

With the exception of Mars all the other outer planets move fairly slowly against the backdrop of the stars and their orbital periods also reflect how long they appear to take to move completely round the ecliptic. Here are the orbital periods of the outer planets in years: Jupiter 11.9, Saturn 29.5, Uranus 84, Neptune 165 and Pluto 248. You might just get to see Uranus complete one orbit in one lifetime but Neptune and Pluto - forget it! The various positions an outer planet has with respect to the Earth is shown in the diagram at right. All outer planets are known as '**Superior Planets**'. Like the inferior planets, when a superior planet lies behind the Sun it is in Conjunction and so cannot be seen. Although the planet is moving slowly against the background stars it is the motion of the Earth around the Sun that decides how well it can be seen. At Quadrature the outer planet is at an elongation from the Sun of 90° and in a telescope the planet doesn't appear to be fully illuminated as in the view I took of

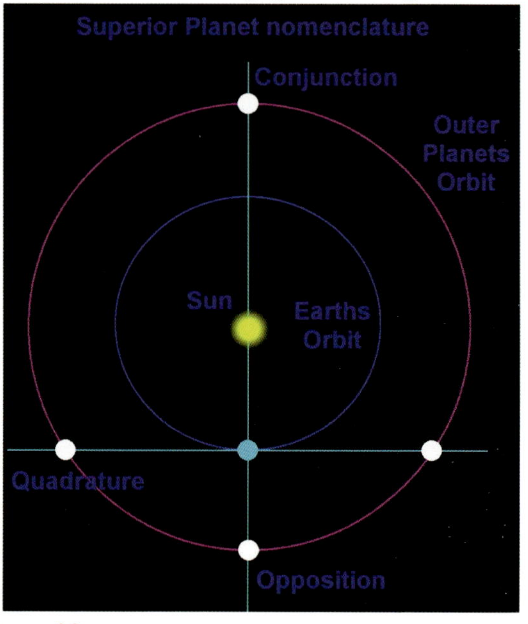

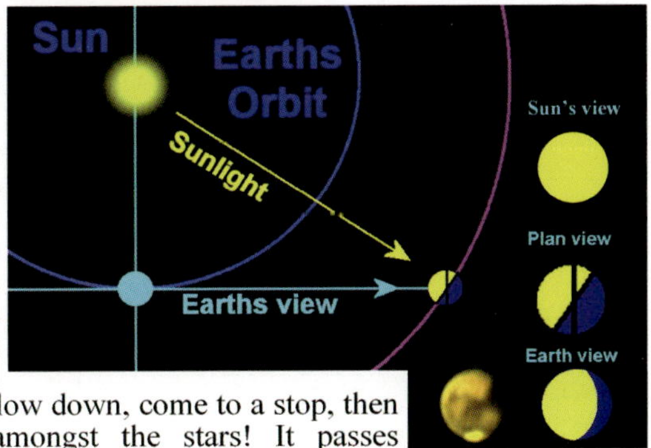

Mars shown here at right. The further out the planet lies though, the less the effect is apparent so that Uranus and Neptune tend to appear fully illuminated almost all the time.

Following the steady motion of the planets against the background stars can be a rewarding project and it soon becomes apparent that the outer planets have a special and strange looking motion as they approach and pass Opposition. Initially the planet has a steady or **'Normal'** motion heading eastwards along the ecliptic but careful observation shows that the planet begins to slow down, come to a stop, then begin to move backwards (westwards) amongst the stars! It passes Opposition during this time and then slows to a halt again before resuming normal, eastwards motion. This strange effect is known as **Retrograde** motion and is an effect due to the inner planet (our Earth in this case) faster motion gradually catching up with, and overtaking, the outer planet. In the case of Mars it can appear as a large loop or a zig zag against the stars. This is due to the closeness of the planet to us, the inclination of its orbit, and where the position of greatest inclination of its orbit occurs along our ecliptic.

Think of it like this: next time you are on the Motorway notice the positions of the cars/lorries against the background hills (or any distant features for that matter). If you are on the inside lane on your own then the background hills etc movie steadily backwards as you drive forwards. Now imagine you are in the middle lane overtaking a slower car. Make sure the driver is concentrating on the road and let you do the observing! From your perspective the car on the inside lane appears to move backwards compared with the background hills as you overtake it. Of course the inner car is not really travelling backwards but your car is the one moving faster so it looks like it does - it's all a matter of perspective and point of view. From their inner perspective you are clearly travelling faster than them as your position changes quickly as you overtake. So Earth is moving faster than Mars (and is in a smaller orbit as well) so it catches up and overtakes the slower moving Mars.

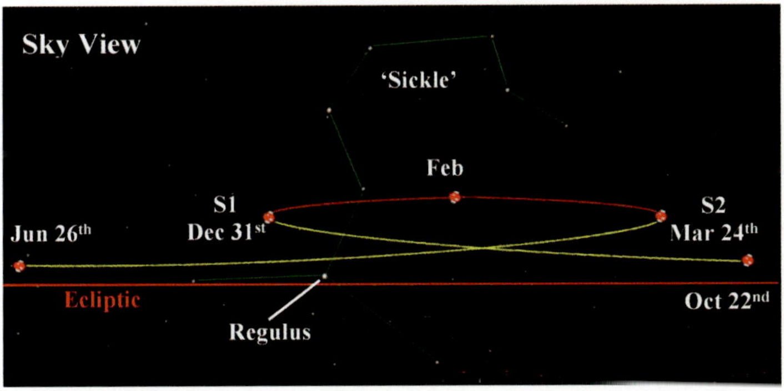

Above is a chart of the Retrograde loop of Mars for late 1994 to mid 1995. The inclination of the Martian orbit to the ecliptic was almost at its greatest and so we get a true loop occurring above the main red line of the ecliptic. The backdrop is the 'sickle' part of the constellation of Leo the Lion with its brightest star Regulus very close to the ecliptic. Mars enters the view in late October 1994 and gradually slows until it reaches its first Stationary Point (S1) which occurred on December 31st. It then appeared to move backwards against the stars passing opposition on February 12th 1995. It continued to retrograde until it slowed down to a second Stationary Point on March 24th (S2) and thereafter resumed normal motion passing just north of Regulus in late May and reaching the edge of our chart by late June. So the retrograde motion is simply the

February Night Sky

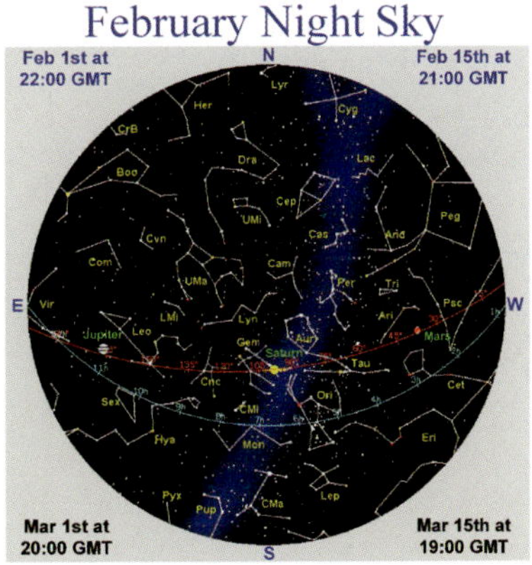

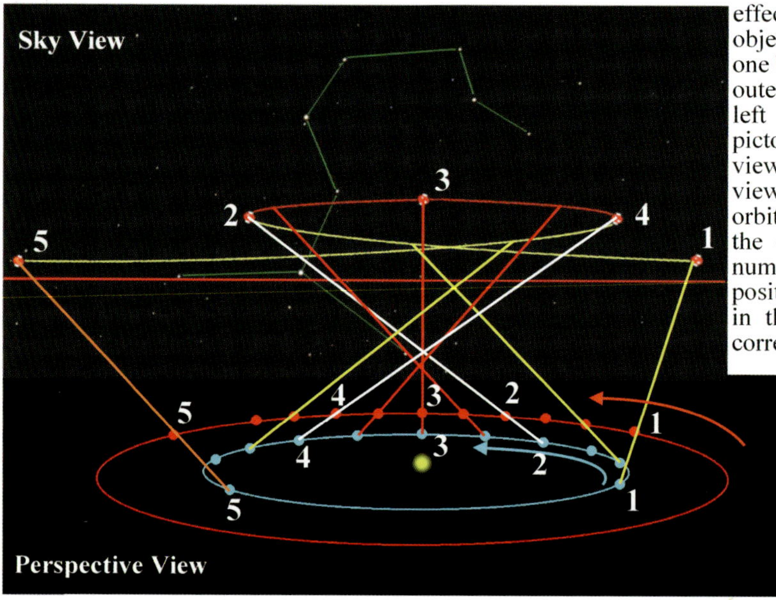

effect of two moving objects, with the inner one being faster than the outer. The diagram at left tries to show this pictorially from the sky view we see and the view looking at the orbits from just above the ecliptic plane. The numbers indicate the positions of the planets in their orbits and the corresponding position against the background sky.

Now move ahead ten years to late 2005 into early 2006 and Mars does a zig zag in the sky instead of a loop - why? This time we are further round our collective orbits when Opposition occurs (see page 19). The tilt of the Martian orbit with respect to the ecliptic means opposition occurs close to one of its crossing points - known as a 'node'. There are always two nodes, one ascending and the other descending as they describe the direction of the Martian orbit and whether it is heading above or below the ecliptic. In the case below Mars starts during August 2005 lying ***below*** the ecliptic. It reaches its first stationary point in October and begins to retrograde. Opposition occurs on November 7th but it crosses the ecliptic at its Ascending Node (marked by the yellow circles) on November 15th before reaching its second Stationary point in December. It then resumes normal motion and lies ***above*** the ecliptic reaching its Descending Node on Dec 3rd 2006. Mars shows the greatest variation of the outer planets because it lies closer to the Earth than them but the same basic ideas apply to them all. You find that the further the planet lies away then the retrograde loop or zig zag gets smaller and if the inclination of the outer planet is small it gives rise to a shallower effect as well.

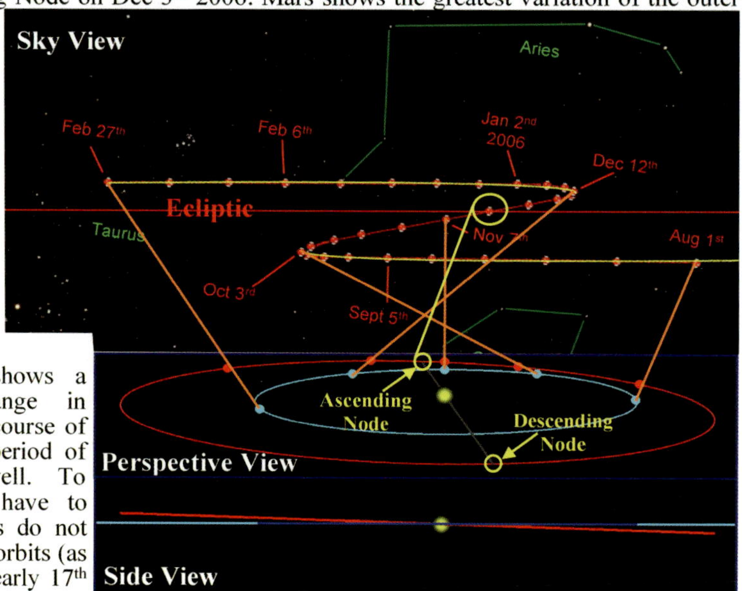

Mars also shows a very noticeable change in brightness during the course of its orbit ***and*** over a period of several years as well. To understand this you have to realise that the planets do not have perfectly circular orbits (as Kepler realised in the early 17th Century). This includes the

Earth and as such there will be times when an opposition occurs favourably and others that are very poor in terms of the brightness and disk size in a telescope. We'll keep to Mars as it is a very good example of this. The ideal opposition is when Earth is at its furthest from the Sun and at the same time Mars is at its closest (to the Sun). This gives us the smallest distance between the two planets and makes Mars brightest and have the largest apparent disk to observe in a telescope as

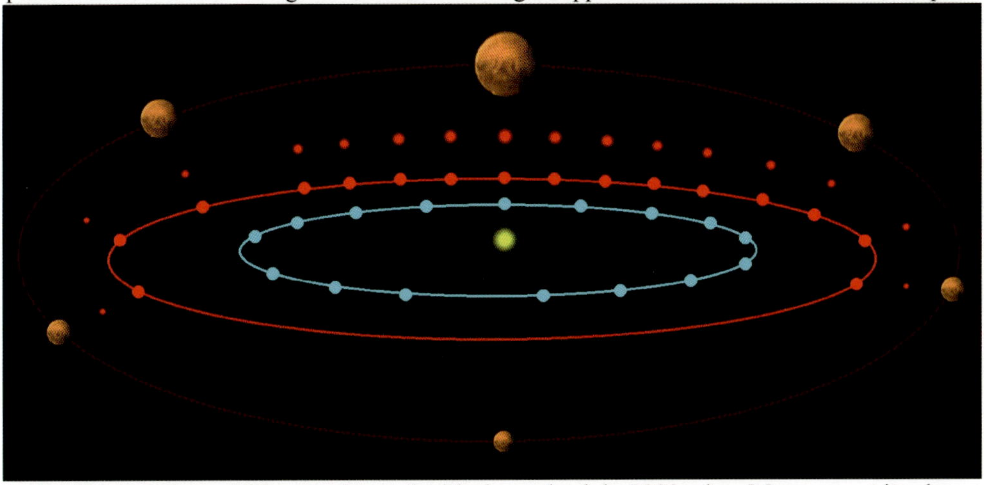

in the diagram above. This was almost the ideal case back in 2003 when Mars was at its closest to Earth than in the last 60,000 years which is why the media paid so much attention. First of all though lets look at how the brightness of Mars changes as the distance decreases between it and Earth. The above diagram shows a perspective view of the orbits of the two planets and just outside the Mars orbit is a series of red disks that gradually get larger as Mars approaches opposition, then they get smaller as the planet recedes from us. Naturally when the distance is greatest between them then Mars will appear small and therefore fainter, conversely when Mars is at opposition it is closer to us and so appears bigger and brighter. The outer real images show the effect of the changes in distance on the disk size seen in a telescope and again when the disk size is small the planet appears faint and when it is large the planet is brighter.

So far so good. The orbits of Mars and Earth are not circular and this can have an effect on whether a particular opposition is bright with a large disk size or a poor one with an average brightness and fairly poor disk size. The following diagram on page 20 shows what I mean. This shows 30 years of Oppositions of Mars from 1988 until 2018 which also represents 2 cycles of Mars oppositions (orange dates and arrows indicate the first cycle and the green dates/arrows are the second cycle concluding with the purple date/arrow). It should be immediately apparent that some oppositions are far better than others. In particular note the dates when the best oppositions occur. They all lie on the side of the orbit that oppositions occur from mid Summer through to late Autumn. Poor oppositions always occur in the Winter and Spring skies (for the Northern Hemisphere). We can conclude then that when Mars is at opposition from Summer to Autumn then it will have the best disk size and be at its brightest it can possibly be. This occurred in 1986 and 1988, 2003 and 2005 and will again happen in 2018 and 2020. So if you missed Mars in late 2005 - tough - you'll have a 13 year wait - sorry but that's celestial mechanics for you!

The disk sizes and brightness of the other outer planets are also affected similarly but to a lesser extent due to their greater distances from the Earth. In the case of Saturn there is the added factor of the tilt of the planet

March Night Sky

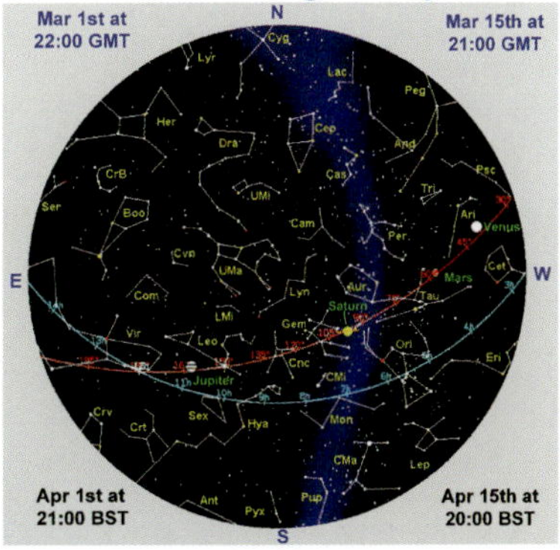

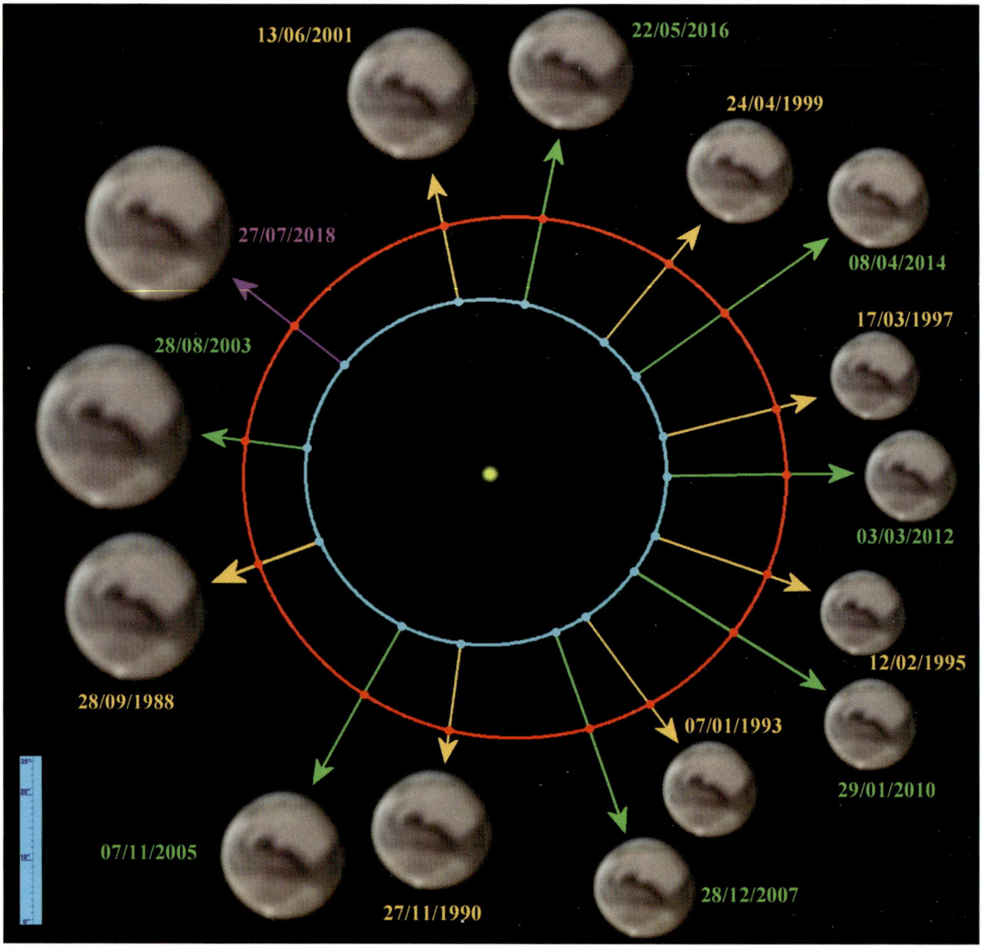

changing how much we see of the ring system which can have a dramatic effect on how bright the planet is. When fully open as in 2003/2004, Saturn was very bright and was very conspicuous against the background stars but in 1995-1996 and again in 2008-2009 the rings will be edge on to our line of sight. Saturn will then be much fainter and will be easier to mistake for just another average brightness star. The pictures below of Saturn show it almost edge on in 1995 (left) and then with the rings almost fully open in January 2005. Note the difference in technology to image the planet, The edge on image was taken using conventional film whilst the better quality image was taken with a webcam. The larger surface area exposed to light from the Sun in the 2005 image makes Saturn look much brighter than back in 1995 when there was little ring surface area to reflect the Suns light.

The Planets and the Ecliptic

As the outer planets gradually make their way round the Sun during the course of their respective 'year' their path against the stars as seen from Earth generally follows the line of the Earths orbit, the Ecliptic. However the various inclinations (tilts) of their orbits to the Ecliptic means that sometimes they can be higher and sometimes lower than the Ecliptic. This creates a

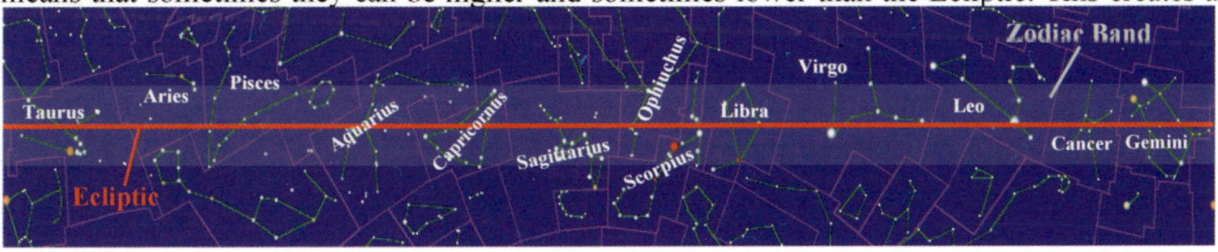

'band' of sky centred on the ecliptic. The constellations that lie along this band are collectively known as the Zodiacal Constellations as shown above. For the two diagrams on this page I have made the Ecliptic straight as, in reality, it is really the Earths orbit extended into space marking the plane that we use to measure the other planets orbital inclination to. Astronomers determine positions in the sky with the equivalent of Latitude and Longitude called **Declination (Dec)** and **Right Ascension (RA)**. They measure RA from the Spring (Vernal) Equinox. This is still referred today as the 'First Point of Aries' as several thousand years ago it did indeed lie in Aries. However, due to an effect called Precession it has slipped back along the ecliptic into neighbouring Pisces. Despite this we generally consider the first constellation of the Zodiac to be Aries followed by: Taurus, Gemini, Cancer, Leo, Virgo, Libra, Scorpius, Sagittarius, Capricornus, Aquarius and finally Pisces. However the Sun following the ecliptic can also pass through a 13th constellation that happens to straddle the ecliptic - Ophiuchus - it lies between Scorpius and Sagittarius. From the Earths perspective the Sun always follows the red line of the Ecliptic, but as mentioned earlier, the planets are inclined to various angles to it so can appear to wander above and below the ecliptic. The largest inclined orbit belongs to Pluto so there are several other constellations that it can 'wander' into over the course of its orbit. This also applies

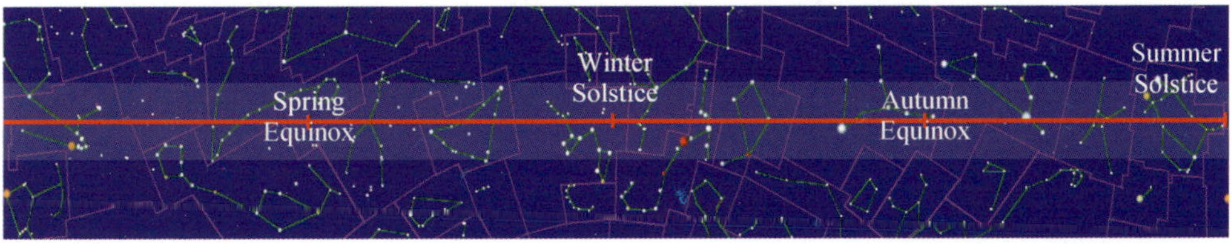

to Mercury and to a lesser extent, Venus, but with Mercury always lingering in a twilight sky you don't tend to notice the background stars or constellation it happens to lie in. From our earth based view the two inner planets are carried along with the Sun as it moves along the ecliptic with them swinging from one side to the other of the Sun. This means they can pass all the planets in turn during the course of a year or so. Mars also moves fairly quickly along the ecliptic but takes around two years to gradually overtake each of the other outer planets. As we look toward the outermost planets their slower motion against the background stars begins to tell. Jupiter will take 11.9 years to move completely round its orbit and so it takes that long to move through all the zodiac constellations and pass the other slower outer planets. Saturn takes 29.5 years, Uranus 84, Neptune 165 and poor Pluto 248 years! The above does not take into account that we are observing from a moving platform (the Earth) which slightly affects the above figures and that during the course of, say the period of Pluto's orbit, all the other planets have moved along the ecliptic as well! So the outer planets are always playing catch up with each

April Night Sky

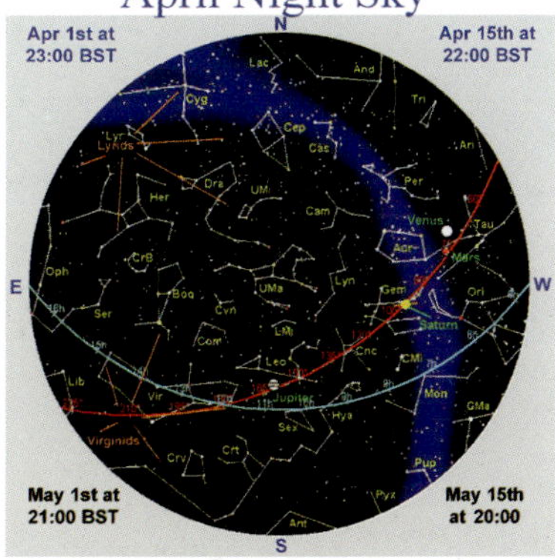

other and it can take centuries for them to appear to group together in the sky.

A good example of this occurred back in Spring 2002. As Mercury swung round the Sun and emerged into the early evening late April sky, it joined Venus, Mars, Saturn and Jupiter to form a 'line of planets' (not strictly a planetary line up though). Unfortunately the author could not photograph this as the weather was very poor but in early May the picture above right was taken from the Algarve, Portugal. By then (May 11th) Venus had crept up and joined Mars as it also slowly moved up past Saturn. This grouping of five bright planets in the evening sky will not be repeated for several centuries and the nearest grouping of four bright planets in the evening sky that will be easily observable occurs in January 2022 (the planets will be Mercury, Venus, Jupiter and Saturn). There will be more groupings of two or three planets in the evening sky in the meantime so keep looking out!

Conjunctions and Occultations

As these planets appear to pass each other on occasions, sometimes it is a close event and others have quite a gap between them. These close encounters are also known as **conjunctions** and can take place between planets, planets and stars, planets and the Moon and a combination of all three events. In the picture above, Venus was in conjunction with Mars. However, technically, true conjunction occurs when the two (or more) objects share the same position in the sky with respect to their RA. Many amateur astronomers though use the term quite loosely and basically call anything that lies close to each other as a conjunction. At left lies two images of Venus and Mars close to each other in the sky on May 10th and 11th 2002. Which is the true conjunction? I would say both are but technically it would be the May 10th image which was taken closest to the time when they shared the same RA in the sky. Therefore conjunctions are not necessarily when the objects are at their closest. The planets can also have conjunctions with the brightest of the Deep Sky Objects such as clusters of Stars and occasionally globular clusters and a few Nebulae as well so these are also pointed out if they are easily visible to either the naked eye or with binoculars. A prime example when Jupiter lay next to Messier 44, the Beehive Cluster in Cancer is shown here at right. It should be noted that Jupiter does not normally have 'spikes' but this was a long guided exposure with the camera aperture stop set at F5.6 giving rise to the spikes! On the next page is an image by the author of a conjunction between Venus and the wonderful naked eye cluster M45, the Pleiades (Seven Sisters) Star Cluster - they were not too far from a bright crescent moon hence the sky looks lighter and bluer (just like the daytime sky).

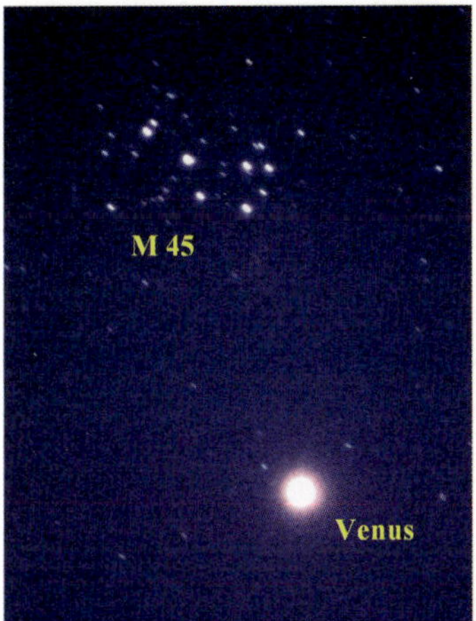

The Moon also has conjunctions with the brighter of the planets (and a few stars as well) and in Nightscenes the best events are mentioned for each month. Again sometimes the gap between the Moon and the planet (or the star) can be close or quite a few degrees away and I tend to mention only the close views as they are the most interesting visually. Shown at right is a view of the Crescent Moon just ¾ degree above Jupiter. Naturally at this scale Jupiter looks just like a star and this view is similar to what would be seen with a pair of 10X50 binoculars - note the day/night boundary on the Moon looks a little crinkled. That's the effect of the craters on the terminator between day and night. An even closer conjunction occurred on January 26th 2002 as shown on the left. This event was so close that to the naked eye it looked as if the Moon had a star attached to it! The view here was taken with my 10" Newtonian telescope and shows the gap between Jupiter and the Moon nicely and the inset shows that one of Jupiter's main cloud belts was also visible. Binoculars could just separate them but naturally a telescope in this case really helped. Further North of where the author observed this event Jupiter actually passed behind the Moon and it was ***occulted*** and this is (naturally) called an **Occultation**. When an asteroid or planet passes in front of a brighter star or the Moon covers a star or planet then it is classed as an occultation and occasionally these events can be viewed with fairly basic equipment. Technically when the Moon passes in front of the Sun in a Total Solar Eclipse (see page 28) then it should really be called an occultation but as it is such a special case it has its own name! There are very few bright naked eye stars that are occulted by either the Moon or a Planet so these events are quite rare and every effort should be made to view them. On January 25th 2006 Saturn occulted the star BY Cancer (BY is the stars designation and is not the word

May Night Sky

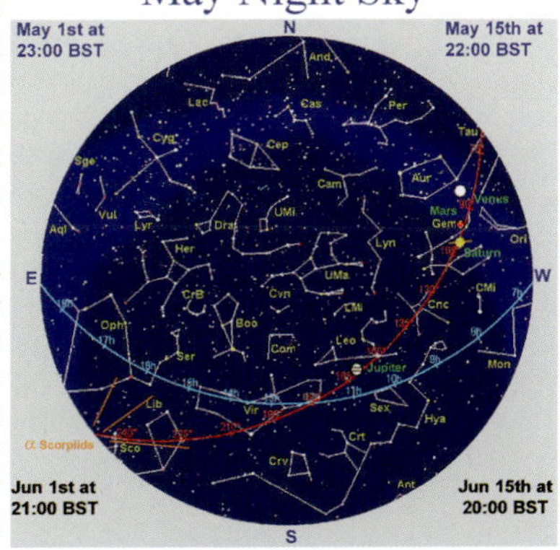

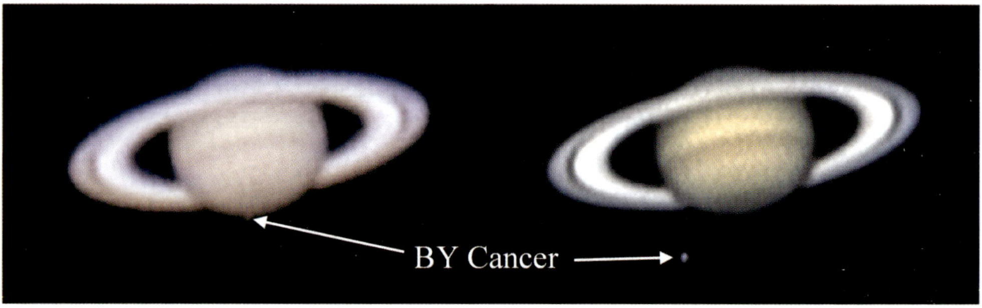

'by') and my images of the emergence of the star is shown above. The left image was taken at 20:53UT and there is a tiny blip just touching the lower part of Saturns disk whilst the right image was taken at 21:30UT with a larger image scale and shows more detail with the star BY Cnc well clear of Saturn.

Deep Sky Objects such as M45 the Pleiades can be occulted by the Moon and December 4th 2006 is a good example of such an event. My diagram at right shows what happens. The almost Full Moon begins the evening off to one side of the cluster but within an hour it starts to cover some of the outlying members of M45. By 4am it covers the main central stars and in the following hour moves off leaving just a couple of the brightest stars occulted.

The Saturn event above did need a telescope to really appreciate but the occultation of M45 is a binocular event so sometimes as long as the sky is clear you do get the chance to view these unusual occurrences. Astronomers use events like these to refine the orbital positions of asteroids, planets and even the Moon and professionals also use the effects of the starlight passing through a planets atmosphere to detect the density of the gas, and often what the gas is made of. Sometimes when the Moon occults a supposedly well known star a surprise can occur, as the star may be found to be a double system if the starlight gradually disappears/reappears rather than abruptly going out/reappearing. Asteroid occultation's are often observed by amateur astronomers as the duration of the star's disappearance gives an estimate of how big the asteroid actually is - something that very few professionals have time to do so they rely on the amateurs to provide the data. There are not many hobbies where you can actually contribute valuable scientific data and it is wanted and appreciated by the professionals!

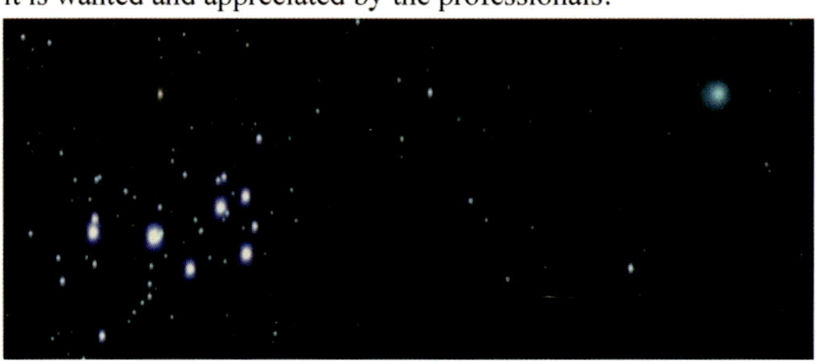

Left: Even Comets can have conjunctions with other objects. Comet Machholz passed M45 during January 2005 and was a fine object in binoculars as imaged here by the Author using a long exposure webcam attached to a 50mm camera lens and tracked using the 10" Newtonian Reflector.

The Moon and its changing phases

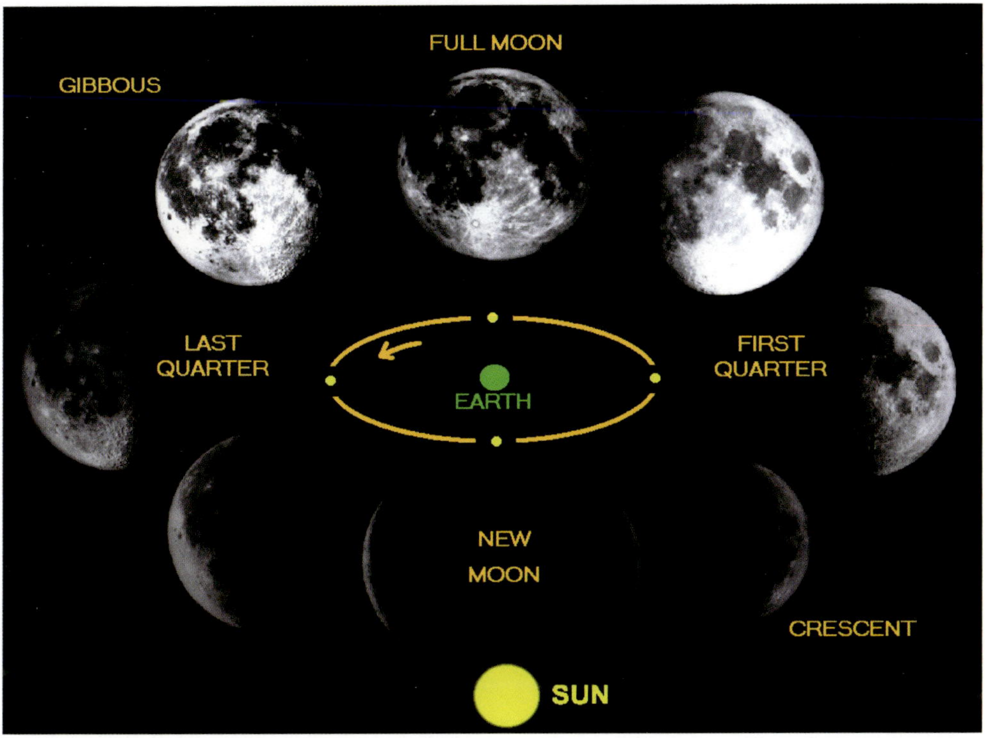

This chart shows the Sun at the bottom with the Earth at centre with the Moon's orbit around it. The large images show the phase seen from the Earth at the corresponding position of the Moon in its orbit. Note: not shown to scale.

During the course of its orbit around the Earth our Moon can be seen to change 'shape' and this often confuses first-time observers who are not familiar with what is happening. When the Moon lies in the same part of the sky as the Sun the sunlit side is turned away from us and we only see the dark side - thus we cannot see it (except during an Eclipse of the Sun) thus we have **'New Moon'**. As the Moon moves along its orbit about the Earth the angle between Earth, Moon & Sun changes so that after seven days it is a right angle and we see the Moon to the left or East side of the Sun. Half of the sunlit side of the Moon is visible and so we see the Moon at **'First Quarter'** (the Moon has travelled the first quarter of its orbit so far).

Another seven days and once again they are back in alignment but this time the Moon is opposite the Sun in the sky & we can now see the sunlit side fully - hence **'Full Moon'**. At this point the Moon will rise just as the Sun sets and the Moon can therefore be seen all night. Seven more days pass and the Moon is once more forming a right angle with the Earth & Sun and we only see half of the sunlit side again - this phase is called the **'Last Quarter'** because there is only the last quarter of the orbit to go. Finally seven days later the Moon is back again at **New**. The diagram overleaf perhaps puts it a little clearer based on our actual ground based view. We shall use a set time of day for each

June Night Sky

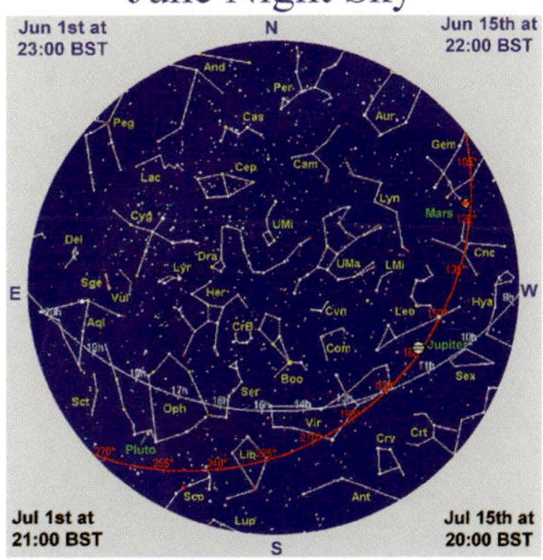

chart which in turn shows ***3 weeks*** worth of Lunar motion at one of the Equinoxes. Chart 1 is set for 6pm and shows the Sun is just setting over in the West. Close to it lies the New Moon effectively setting with it and so it cannot be seen (unless that day it was a Total Solar Eclipse!),

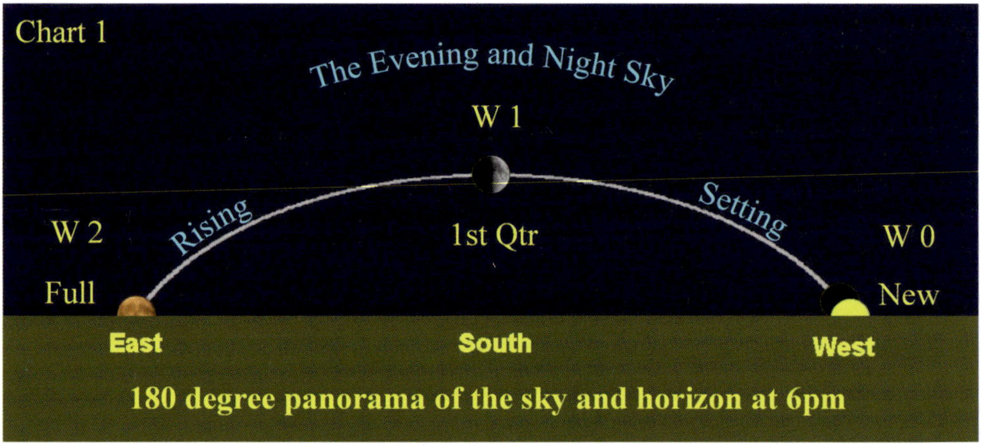

this is on our first week, Week 0 **(W0)**. However ***one week later*** **(W1)** at 6pm the First Quarter Moon (1st Qtr) lies high in the sky due South and so is easily visible. ***Another week later*** **(W2)** the Full Moon is just rising over in the East at 6pm (note the orangey-red colour for effect!) and therefore it is on the other side of our sky from where the Sun sets. From this we can see that depending on which week it is the Moon lies in a different place in the evening sky ***at 6pm on succeeding weeks***.

Now for Chart 2, lets move time on by six more hours to give Midnight. The entire sky now is split in two giving us what's left of the Evening sky over in the West (right) whilst we now

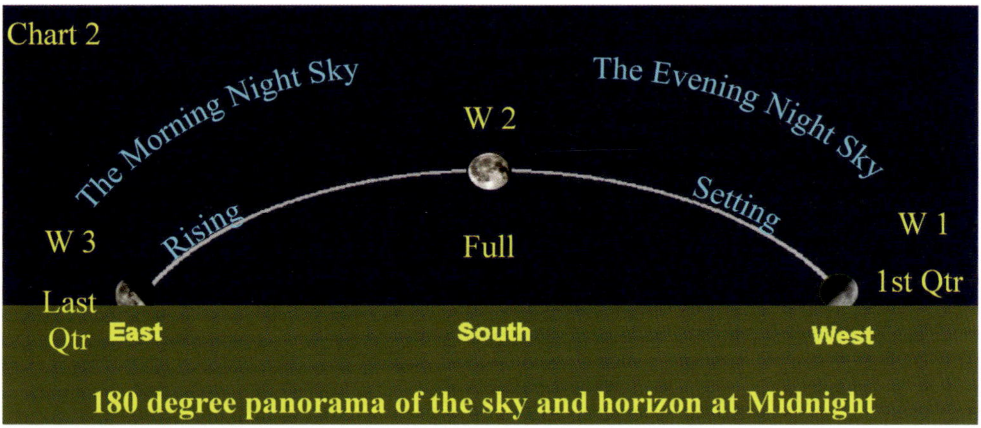

begin to see the stars of the Morning sky over in the East (left). At ***midnight*** the 1st Qtr Moon is setting in the West **(W1).** A week later **(W2)** the Full Moon is due South and dominating the night sky. Another week on **(W3)** and the Last Quarter Moon is just rising over in the East and lies in the Morning Sky, remember all times for this chart are Midnight.

Finally on the next page, Chart 3 takes us six more hours ahead to ***6am***. The Morning sky has the Full Moon setting over in the West **(W2)**. A week later **(W3)** the Last Quarter Moon lies due South at 6am and finally after one more week **(W4)** the New Moon is back next to the Sun rising with it over in the East. If the previous was not clear enough then try looking at the 3 charts like this: Follow what the Moon does over the next twelve hours for that particular phase. On

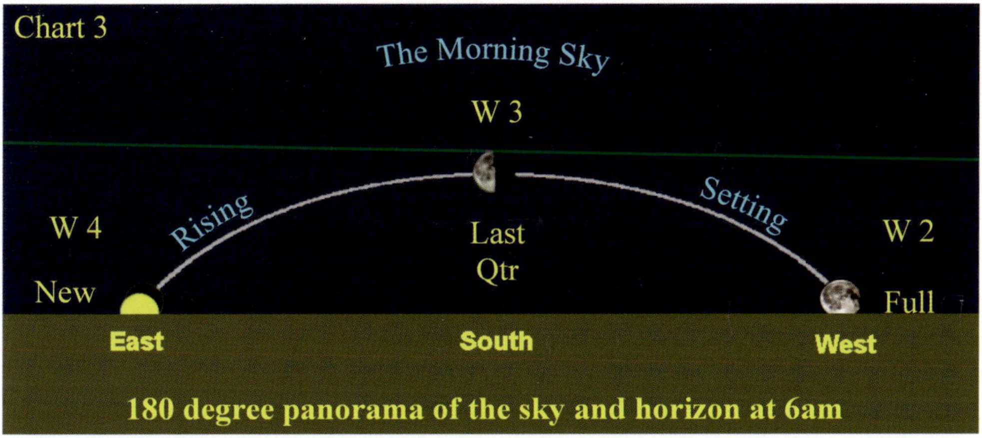

Chart 1 the **Full Moon** is just rising in the East at 6pm. Chart 2 is six hours later (and so it's midnight) and now the Full Moon lies due South whilst Chart 3 is another six hours on (6am) and the Full Moon is now setting in the West. In other words the Moon has crossed the entire sky during the course of the night. This can also be applied to any celestial object in the sky, they rise in the east, travel across the sky during the course of the night then set in the west.

But what about features visible to the naked eye and binoculars? Naked eye allows you to follow the phases during the month with the New to Full moon phases being called 'waxing' and the phases of the moon from Full to New being called 'waning'. The dark patches on the moon known as the Maria are large impact basins that filled with lava that cooled quickly forming a dark volcanic rock called basalt. In some places there appear bright streaks across the moon and these are the ray patterns associated with some of the fresher craters. In particular the rays from Tycho in the southern hemisphere of the Moon is a good example shown here at lower left when the moon is almost fully illuminated. Binoculars bring out more of these features with the craters being especially prominent along the day/night boundary known as the terminator (not to be confused with a certain film series!). A good map of the moon is worth investing in or even using software to help identify the various features and when best to view them.

Two views of the Moon - Crescent and 1st Qtr

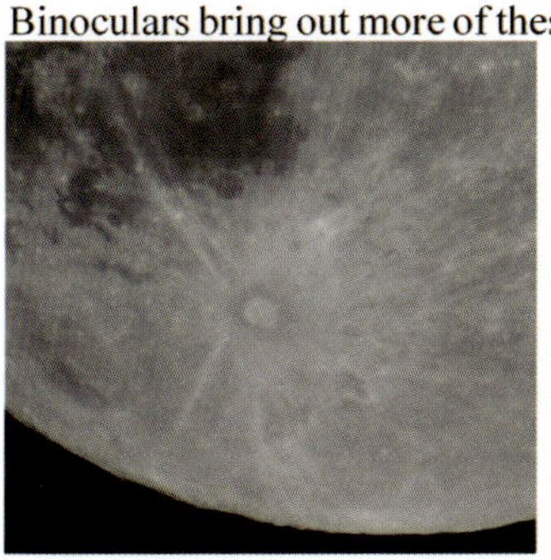

July Night Sky

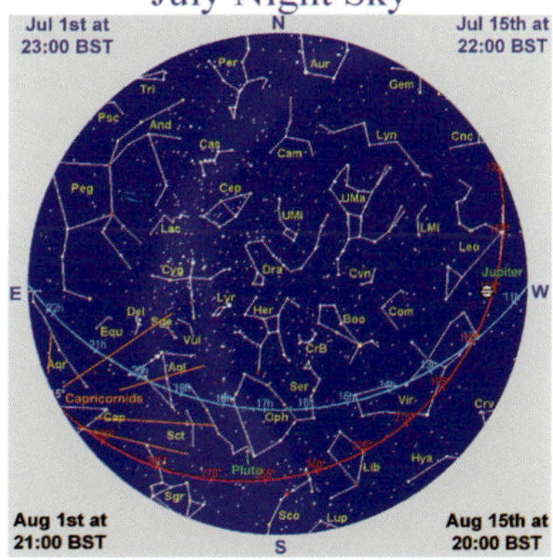

Solar and Lunar Eclipses

Now it follows from the previous pages that as the Moon travels round the Earth in its orbit then there has to be a time when it should pass directly behind the Earth and therefore into its shadow and also two weeks later should pass directly in front of the Sun as well. So we should have an eclipse of the Sun and Moon ***every*** month. Clearly this does not happen and so the real situation involves the orbit of the Moon being tilted with respect to the Earths orbital plane about the Sun. The inclination of the Lunar Orbit to the Ecliptic is 5° as shown below. From this you can

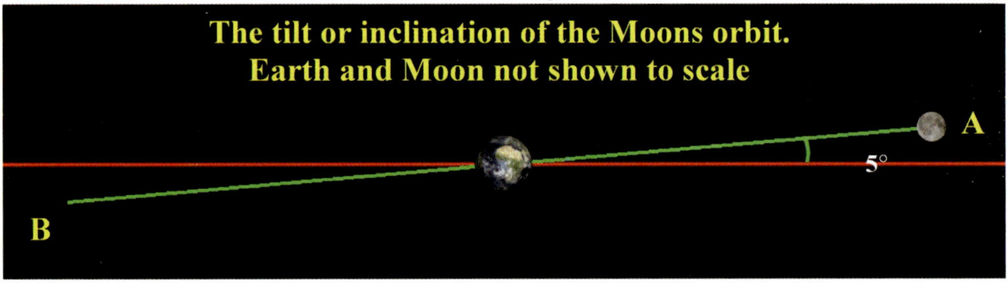

see that when it is on one side the Moon can be above the Earths Ecliptic (A) and two weeks later (B) it can lie below. At these extremes the Moon would miss the Earths shadow/solar disk if they occurred when the tilt and ecliptic line up. So what makes the Lunar tilt and Ecliptic line up? Precession. Lets look at the orbit/ecliptic from a slight angle as shown below. Naturally everything has been exaggerated for clarity. The Moon is shown at four positions around its orbit, at its greatest high/low points and at two crossing points known as Nodes. Node A lies where the orbit of the Moon is ascending above the Ecliptic whilst Node D is the descending part of the orbit with the line connecting them being simply the line of the Nodes. The Nodes are VERY important for us to get eclipses. From the Earths viewpoint the Nodes gradually drift around the Ecliptic and it is when one of the Nodes intersects the position of the Earths shadow or the Solar disk AT THE SAME TIME AS THE MOON then an eclipse can occur. So the Moon has to be at or very close to a node at a critical time in its orbit - either New or Full Moon otherwise there can be no eclipse and it misses the Shadow or the Solar disk. So for most of the time we see no eclipses at all but every so often it all comes together and depending on whether it's Full Moon or New means we get either a **Total Lunar Eclipse** or a **Total Solar Eclipse**. The

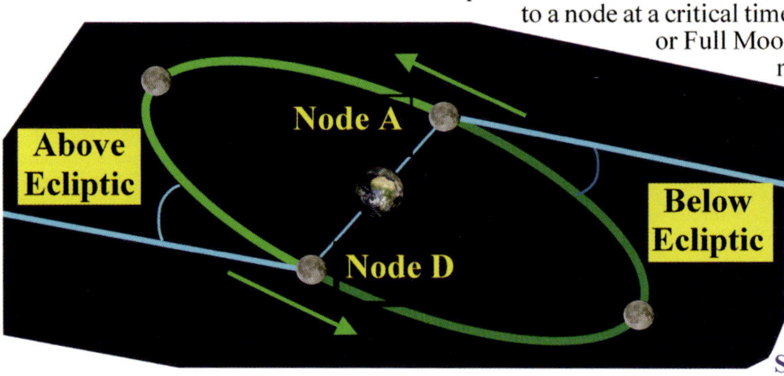

diagram below shows the circumstances for a **Lunar Eclipse** and what we see when one occurs. The diagram is a plan view with the sizes greatly exaggerated and distances not to scale. The Earths shadow has two parts: the Penumbra where part of the Sun is still visible to the Moon and the Umbra when the Moon lies completely inside the Earths shadow. Totality occurs when the

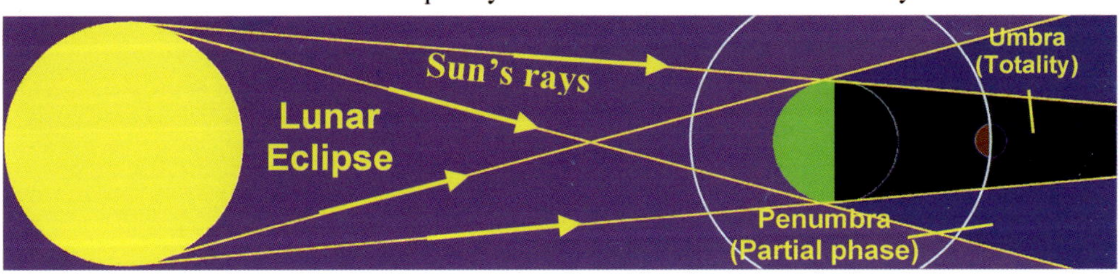

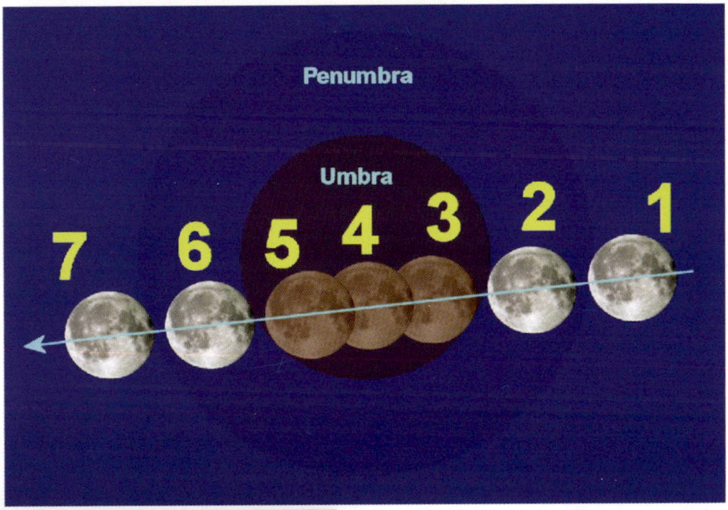

Moon lies inside the Umbra. Therefore the stages of a Lunar eclipse (shown at right) occur like this: at 1 the Moon is just about to enter the Penumbra and at 2 it is just about to enter the Umbra. Because the penumbra only darkens the Moon slightly most people notice the eclipse occurring once stage 2 has begun. Start and end of complete Totality is 3 & 5 with mid Totality at 4. For most observers the end of the eclipse occurs at 6 but really the true end of the eclipse is when the Moon finally leaves the penumbra at 7. The Umbral part of Earths shadow is quite large and so Totality can last over an hour compared with a Solar Eclipse which is just a mere few minutes at most! One thing to look for is the colour of the Moon when it is totally eclipsed as it usually appears either a bright or dull reddish colour as shown at left in my picture. This occurs because the Earth has an atmosphere (for which we are grateful!) and it refracts the sunlight breaking it into the colours of the rainbow. The blue and most of the other colours are scattered away from the umbra but the red tends to be scattered ***into*** the umbra. It is a little more complicated than that but hopefully you get the picture.

Total Lunar Eclipse

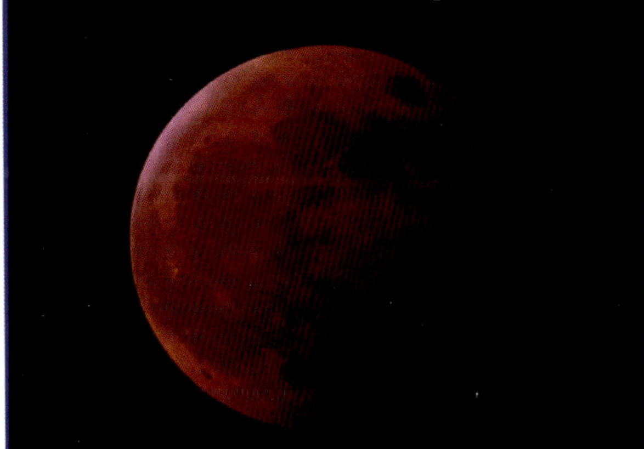

January 9th 2001

Now lets turn to a **Solar Eclipse**. The Sun (and Moons) disk is much smaller than the Earths shadow so the Totality phase is far shorter and as both the Sun and Lunar disks are almost the same apparent size in the sky the actual Totality can last just a few seconds or up to about 8 minutes at its longest. The partial eclipse phase is much longer lasting (either side of Totality) for several hours so you would be forgiven for wondering what all the fuss is about for just a brief Totality! A Total Solar Eclipse is the only natural way for us to view the outer atmosphere

A Partial Lunar Eclipse

taken on September 7th 2006

August Night Sky

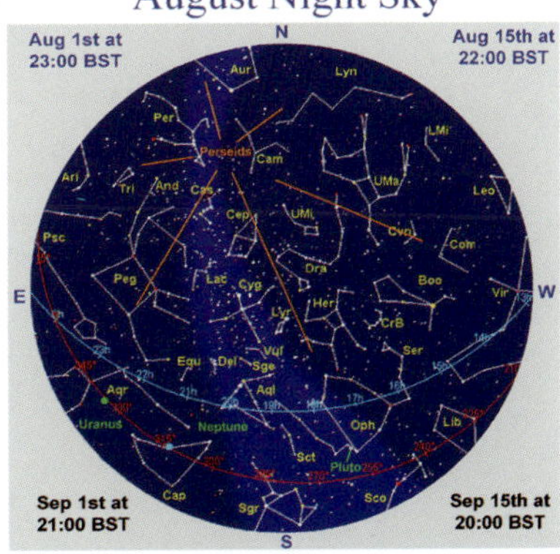

of the Sun, known as the Corona. It is a million times fainter than the Sun so is impossible to see unless you can block out the bright disk of the Sun. That's where the wonderful effect of the Sun and Moons respective sizes and distances comes into play. The Moon is 400 times smaller than the Sun ***BUT*** the Sun happens to lie 400 times further away so from our viewpoint on the Earth it looks like they have the same size disk on the sky! The typical Total Eclipse sequence of start, mid and finish is shown here with a real view of the actual Total Solar Eclipse the author imaged in Turkey on March 29th 2006 shown at centre. The plan view of what happens is shown below. The track of Totality is only a few

hundred miles wide and quickly crosses the Earths surface because of the combined motions of the Earth turning on its axis and the Moons orbital motion as it moves around our planet. So if you want to see Totality then you really have no choice but to be somewhere along (and preferably at the centerline) of the track. Outside this and you will see varying degrees of a partial eclipse similar

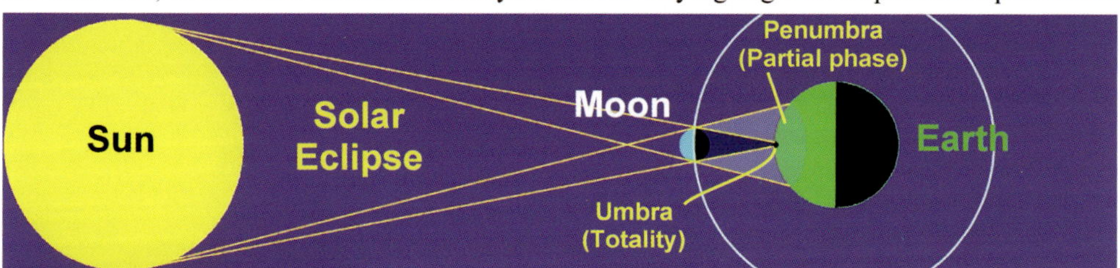

to the view shown below at left which took place on May 31st 2003.

However the Moons orbit is not perfectly circular and so the Moons apparent size can vary depending on its distance from the Earth when Totality occurs. When the size of the Moons disk is slightly bigger than the Suns then you will have a short duration for Totality of just seconds, whilst if the Moon is closer to the Earth then it will appear bigger and so give a longer Totality lasting several minutes. If the Moon happens to be at its furthest point from the Earth at Totality then the disk is smaller than the Suns and you get what's called an annular eclipse where, at mid totality, there is a ring of light around the edge of the Moon (the

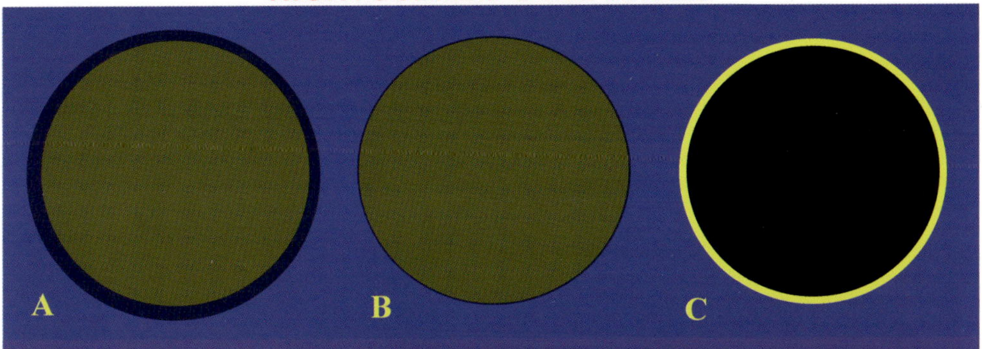

A: Moon closer and bigger - longer totality. B: Moon/Sun almost same size very short totality. C: Moon further and smaller so Annular Eclipse seen.

annulus) which is the edge of the Suns disk still visible. The diagram above illustrates this, note in A and B the Moon has been made semi transparent in order to see the size of the Solar Disk behind. Just at the start and end of Totality you may see what's called the 'Diamond Ring Effect'. This is where the last light of the solar disk shines through a deep valley on the limb of the Moon. It can be quite dramatic to see and at right is my view of the Diamond Ring at the start of the March 29th 2006 Totality seen from Turkey. There are many other subtle effects to look out for during a total Solar Eclipse but these are well beyond the scope of this book and the Author urges everyone to make the effort to view at least one Total Solar Eclipse during their lifetime - it's an experience that is truly unforgettable.

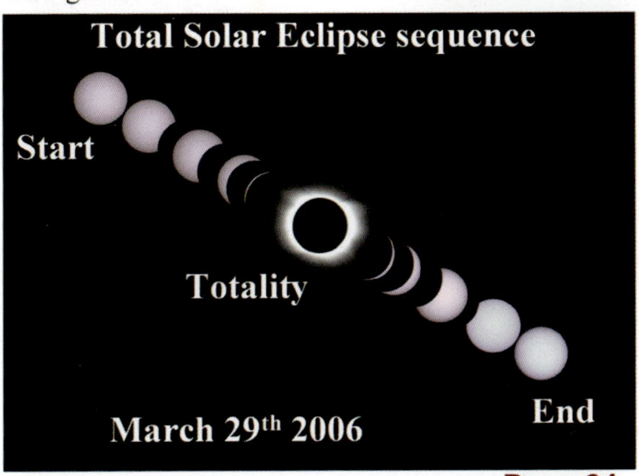

September Night Sky

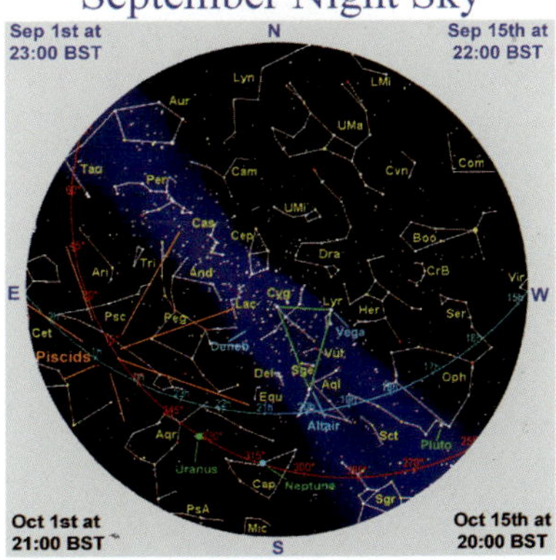

Constellations of the Northern Hemisphere

We have talked about many things in this book but perhaps the first thing to be really learnt is the main constellations. I use several as guideposts to the others and so here are the main constellations arranged by season and starting with the Circumpolar constellations as they can be viewed all year round. Note that not all the constellations are shown due to the limitations of this book and those shown are not to the same scale. Constellations that are circumpolar are shown inside the yellow circle and include: Ursa Minor and Ursa Major, Draco, Cameleopardalis, Cepheus, Cassiopeia, Lacerta, Lynx and Canes Venatici. It also includes a large part of the following: Andromeda, Perseus, Auriga and some of Cygnus. Bright stars that are circumpolar include Capella, Deneb and Vega.

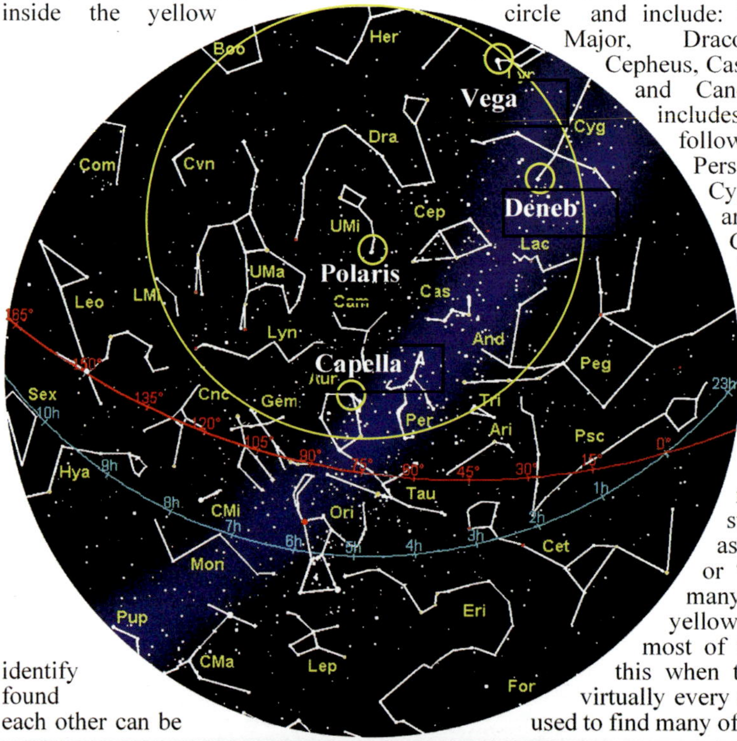

Ursa Major - otherwise known as the Great Bear, is so easily recognizable that it is the best constellation to use to find many others as shown below. The main brightest seven stars make up the asterism of the 'plough' or 'saucepan' amongst its many names (shown in yellow on the next page) and most of the public can usually identify this when the sky is clear. Once found virtually every angle the stars make to each other can be used to find many of the main constellations

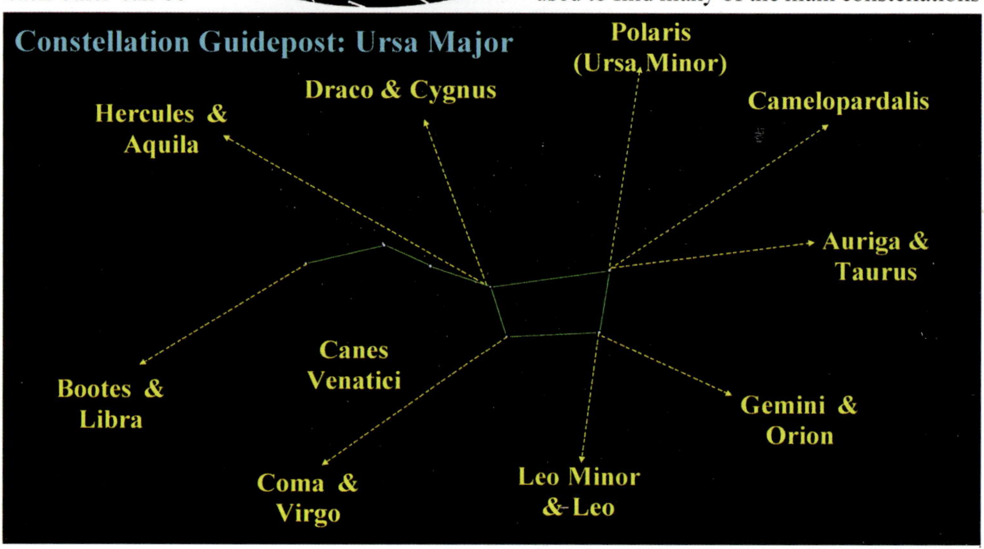

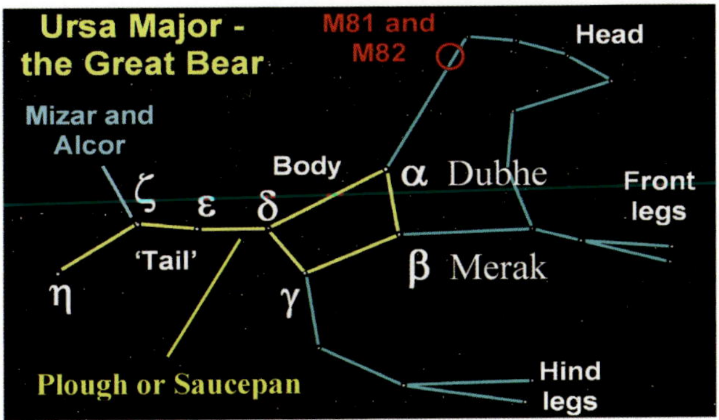

as shown earlier. Ursa Major is the Latin name for the 'Great Bear' and certainly it looks like some sort of animal when you include the fainter stars as well. Ursa Minor or the Little Bear is seen at lower left and as mentioned on page 8 has the Northern Hemisphere's pole star - Polaris. Polaris is a double star in small telescopes so don't just line your telescope up on it - take a look at it as well!

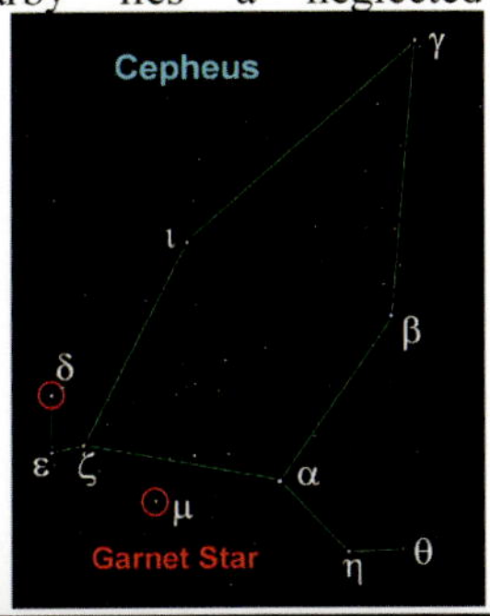

Nearby lies a neglected constellation - Cepheus the King. It has two interesting stars in particular. Delta is the prototype of the Delta Cepheids variable stars - valuable for working out the scale of the Universe whilst Mu (μ)Cep is a very red star nicknamed the Garnet star - see what you think as it is naked eye but more easily visible in binoculars. Cassiopeia is the Queen but is best recognized by its 'W' or 'M' shape (depending on the time of evening/year you look). Take a line from **α** to **β** and continue for a little more than the same distance and in binoculars you should find a nice hazy cloud which is the open cluster M52. A smaller but slightly brighter and looser cluster is M103 lying near to **δ** and to make this area more enjoyable the Milky Way passes through the constellation as well. Perseus the Hero (right) also has the Milky Way running through it and so has many things to view with just a few highlighted here such as the wonderful 'Double Cluster' (directly between Perseus and Cassiopeia), the large 'O-B' association of stars including α Per. **β** Per (Algol) is nicknamed the Demon star as it is an eclipsing binary and fades by just over a magnitude every 2 ¾ days and is observable to the naked eye whilst not too far away lies the open cluster, M34.

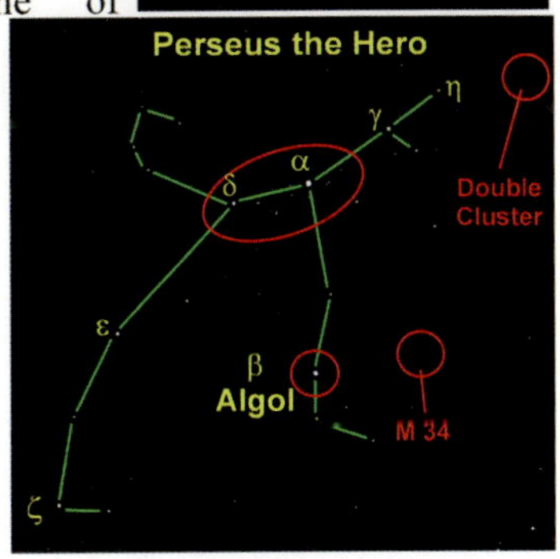

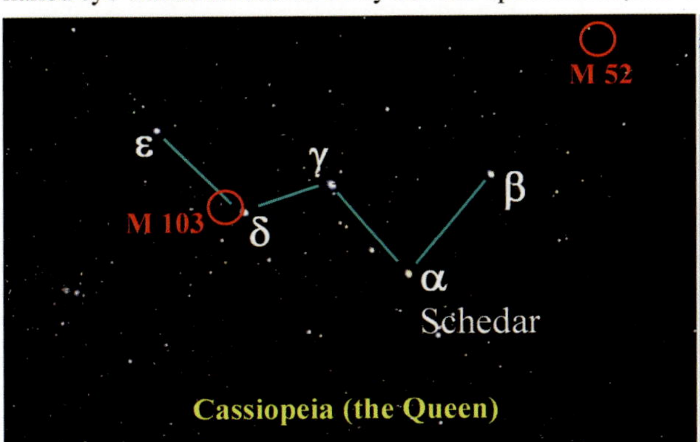

October Night Sky

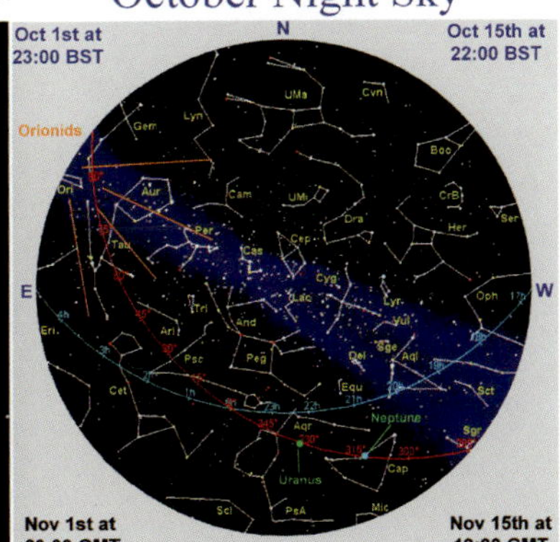

The Autumn Constellations

Andromeda (the Princess) and Pegasus (the flying Horse) lead the way with Pegasus being a good constellation to act as a guidepost (right). The main part of Pegasus is the 'Square' but overall the constellation has little for the casual observer except for the bright globular cluster M15 but nearby Andromeda more than makes up for its neighbour with the marvellous Andromeda Galaxy, M31. It is the brightest and nearest naked eye galaxy in our skies lying an estimated 2.3 million light years away! Aquarius (the Water Carrier) lies the opposite side of Pegasus to Andromeda and is a sprawling constellation but does have a great globular cluster - M2 as well as two other Messier objects, M72 another fainter globular and the small asterism of M73. The right hand stars of the Square of Pegasus point down to Aquarius but continue on until you reach a fairly bright and isolated star - this is Fomalhaut in Pisces Austrinus (the Southern Fish). Fomalhaut is known to have a dusty disk around it so you never know there may be planets forming around that star! It always lies low above the horizon during the autumn and is fairly easy to locate using Pegasus.

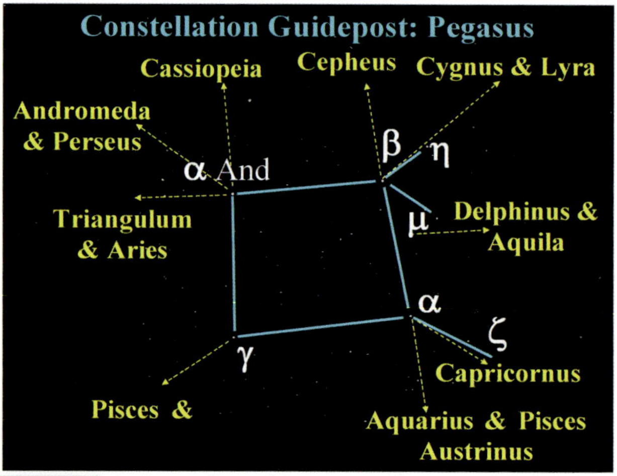

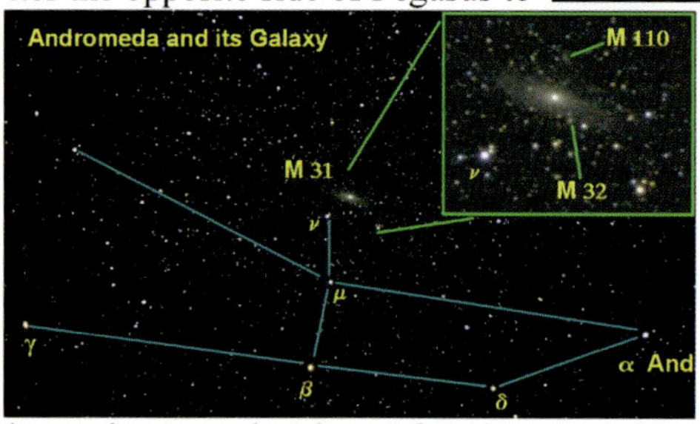

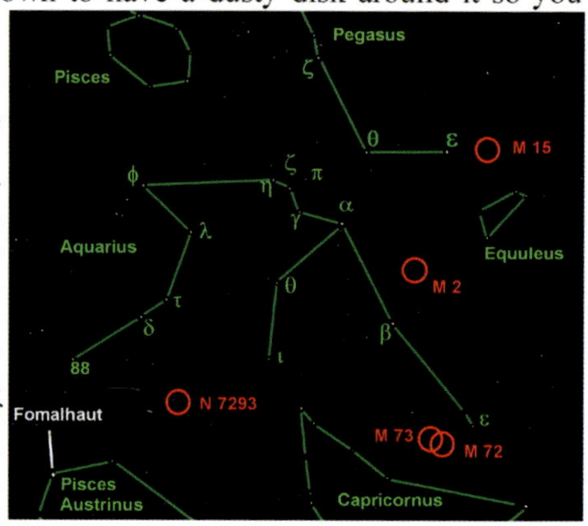

Pisces (the Fishes) seems to linger under Pegasus and is a fairly long constellation with little for the naked eye but it does currently hold the position of the Vernal (Spring) Equinox and it does point the way down to Cetus the Whale. Cetus has the prototype of a long period variable star in the form of Mira (the wonderful) which is a bright variable star taking over 330 days to vary most of which can be followed using the naked eye and binoculars. There are two Messier galaxies (M74 in Pisces and M77 in Cetus) in this region but they are fairly faint for the casual observer but are marked on the chart at left. Despite looking quite unremarkable Triangulum (the Triangle) has a saving grace with the Galaxy M33. The galaxy is best found using binoculars and extending a line down from M31 to β Andromeda and continuing on almost the same distance again. M33 is a face on galaxy making it harder to spot in telescopes but seems reasonably good as a faint 'cloud' in binoculars. Nearby Aries the Ram holds nothing decent for the naked eye/binoculars but it is a zodiacal constellation and used to have the Vernal Equinox until precession carried it into Pisces.

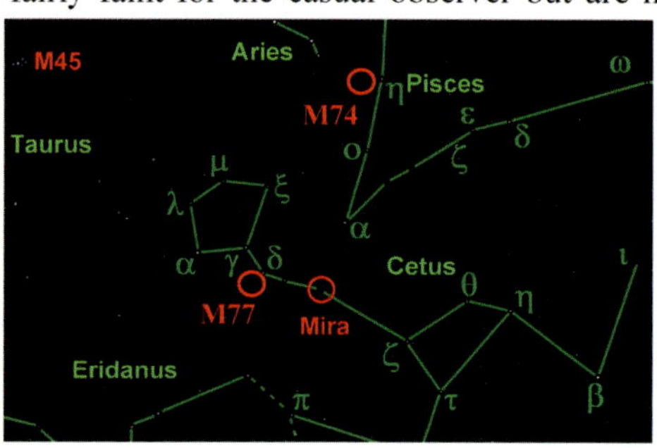

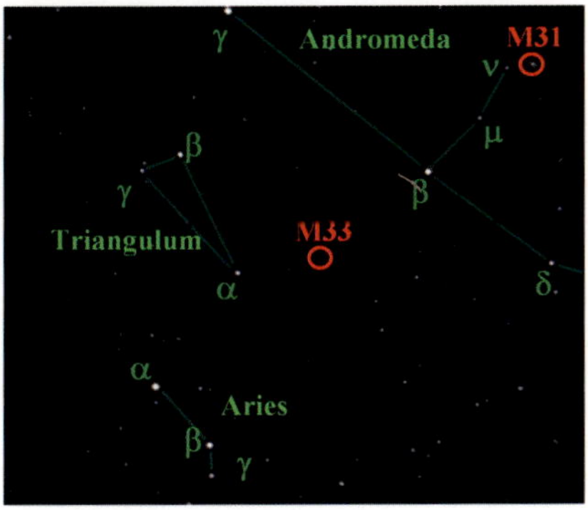

The Winter Constellations

By late Autumn the eastern skies hold several constellations representing the next season and once Cetus is well visible it's not long before Taurus (the Bull) and Orion (the Hunter) become well placed to view. Orion is the Winter skies guidepost and is shown below. It has to be one of the most dramatic constellations with so many bright stars dominating its shape. Of particular note is Betelgeuse (α Ori) which is a bright orange/red supergiant star, the belt of Orion - a line of three stars and the Sword of Orion which hangs down below the belt and contains a wonderful patch of misty light known as the Orion Nebula - M42/43. Orions belt can be used to point up to Taurus or downwards to Canis Major (the Great Dog). Taurus holds several deep sky objects some of which are easily seen with the naked eye such as M45, a bright open cluster also called the Pleiades or Seven Sisters. Forming the head of the Bull is the large open cluster the Hyades with the brightest star **α** Tau called Aldebaren as the blazing red eye of the Bull. However Aldebaren is only half the distance of the cluster so is not a true member just a line of sight effect. ζ (zeta) and **β** (beta) Tau are the bulls horns and just above ζ lies a quite faint patch of light in binoculars which is the supernova remnant the Crab Nebula, M1. Auriga, the Charioteer, has the bright star Capella which is actually circumpolar and three good open clusters of M38, M36 and M37 as shown below. Meanwhile Gemini the Twins (next page) lies further down from Auriga and also has a good cluster in M35 whilst the stars Castor and Pollux appear quite different with white and yellow coloured stars respectively. Canis Major (overleaf) has the distinction of having the brightest star of the entire sky - Sirius, the Dog star. It lies just 8.7 light years away so is relatively close to us hence its brightness. Below it lies another open cluster worthy of attention with binoculars so take a look at M41.

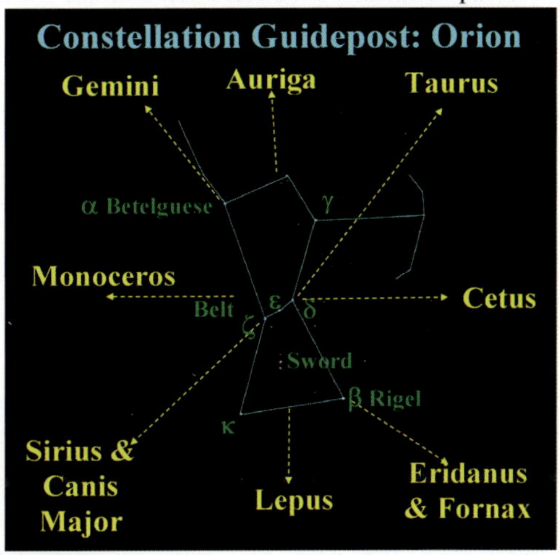

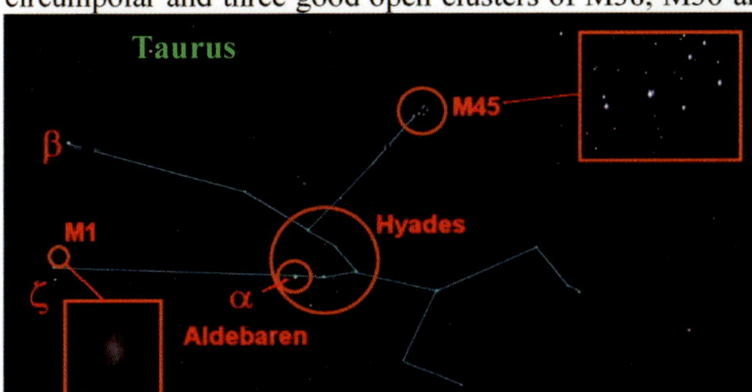

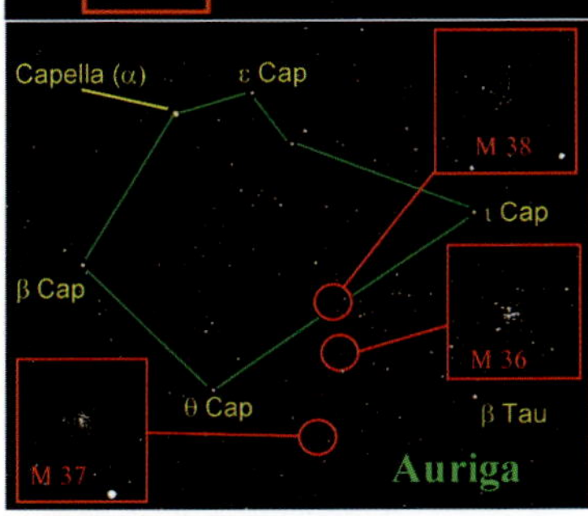

November Night Sky

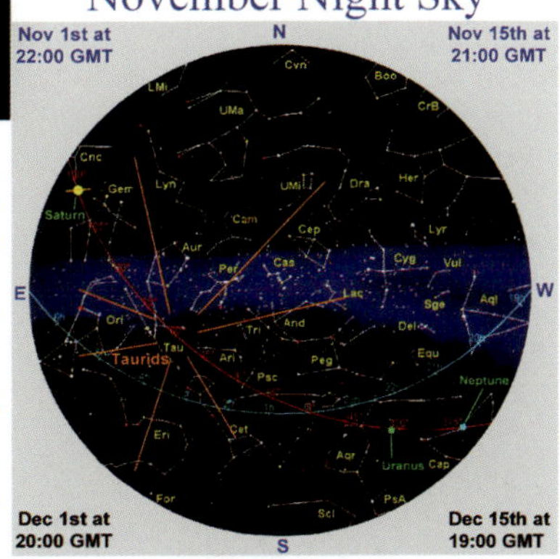

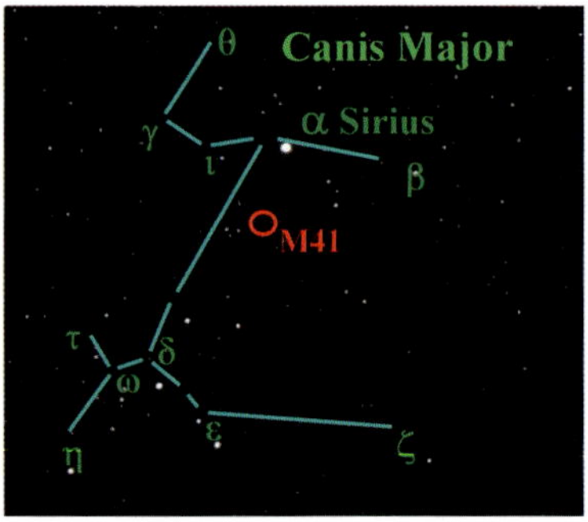

The Spring Constellations

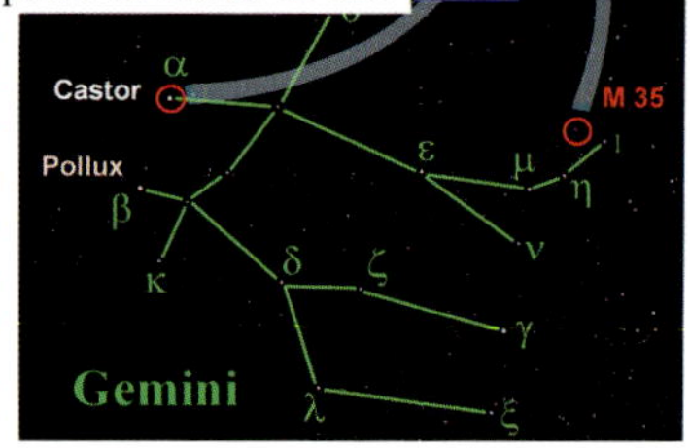

As Taurus and Orion head over to the west during March then we can turn our attention out into deep space as most of the Spring Constellations have Galaxies amongst their stars. The guidepost constellation for this season is Leo the Lion (below). Leo has quite a distinct shape made up of a backwards question mark and a triangle on its left side. The bright star Regulus marks the end of the question mark and is often a star that can lie close to the Moon and so features regularly in Nightscenes. There are five Messier objects, M65&66, M95&96 and M105 all galaxies, in this constellation but they do require careful hunting down in binoculars. However Messier missed a brighter galaxy near the top of the close to λ (Lambda) Leo and it is called NGC 2903 so look for a small misty patch here. Virgo (the virgin) and Coma Berenices (Bernices' Hair) are to the left (east) of Leo and it is here we find one of the richest concentrations of galaxies that the amateur astronomer can hunt down as the area between them is called the 'Realm of the Galaxies'. I have shown two of the Messier objects M84 & M86 (both galaxies) but there isn't room for all of them as there are at least 18 from Coma down into Virgo! Spica is another bright star that sometimes has the Moon close to it so do look out for those conjunctions (see page 22). To the east of Coma lies Bootes the herdsman and Corona Borealis, the Northern Crown - charts for this and Hercules on the next page. Although fairly bright there is no easy deep sky object in them but follow a line from the bright, orange star Arcturus up towards Canes Venatici (the hunting dogs) and you can find a bright-ish globular here - M3. Meanwhile near to the top of Bootes and Corona lies Hercules the strongman which despite the rich mythology surrounding him has quite faintish stars marking his shape. However it makes up for it with the Northern Hemispheres best globular - M13 which is fairly easy to identify as it has two stars flanking it to guide you. While you're there though do check out its fainter and smaller neighbour of M92 - very often missed and neglected due to its bigger and brighter cousin.

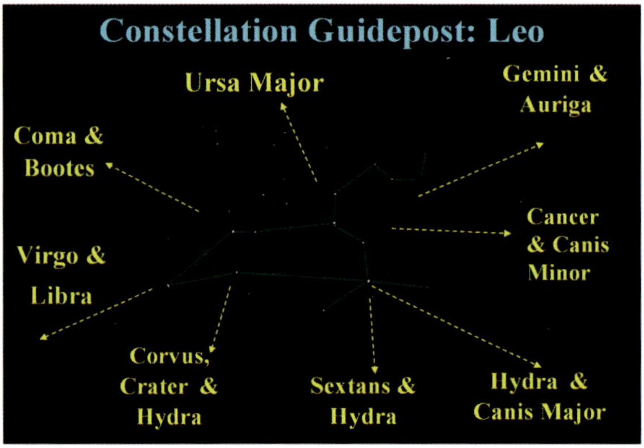

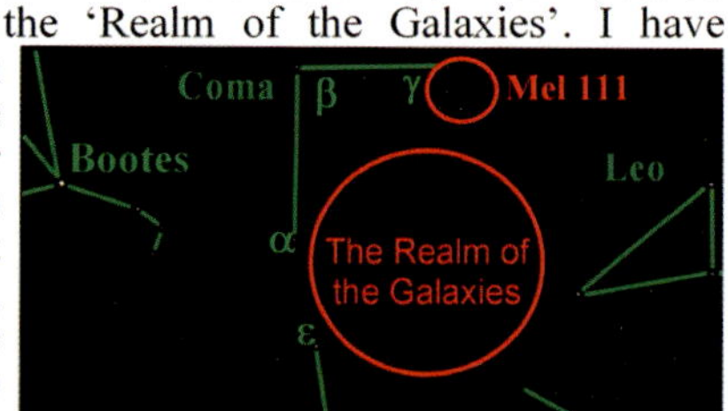
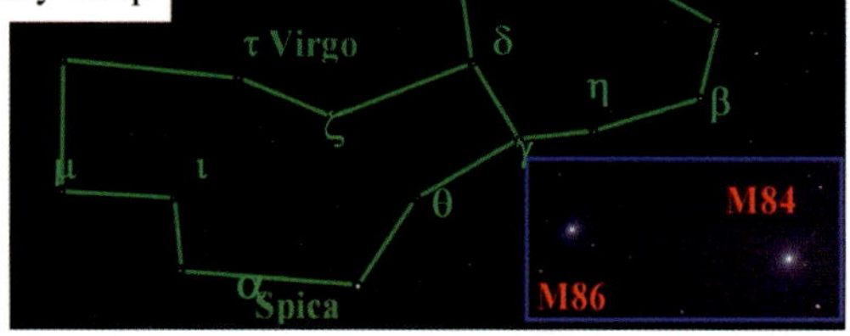

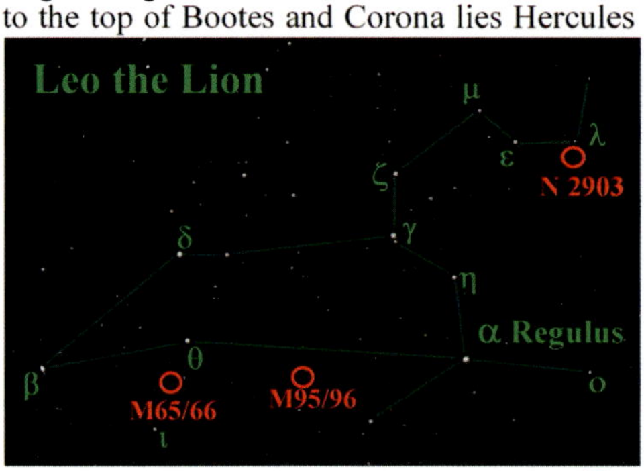

The Summer Constellations

With Hercules high in the sky the Summer constellations now make an appearance. Cygnus and Lyra dominate with Aquila below them. Their brightest stars, Deneb, Vega and Altair, form the famous 'Summer Triangle' (at right), a term coined by the great TV populariser of Astronomy, Sir Patrick Moore. As can be seen at left Cygnus makes a great guide to the rest of the nearby constellations and has the wonderful colourful double star, Albireo for its head. Many other jewels lie in it including two Messier open clusters, M39 & M29 whilst Lyra nearby includes the famous Double Double star system of Epsilon (ε) Lyrae and the small but bright planetary nebula M57, the 'Ring Nebula'. Following the direction of the long 'stem' of Cygnus downwards past Albireo takes you along the galactic plane, rich in deep sky objects. Aquila is the Eagle (below centre) and has surprising little for casual observers but as you enter Scutum, Serpens and down into Sagittarius then the rich star clouds become evident as shown here at lower left. Binoculars will show a host of objects such as M16 & M17 (nebulae) the Starcloud M24, Star

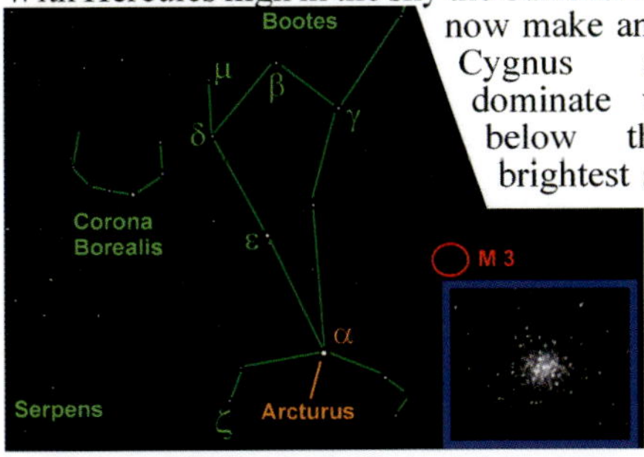

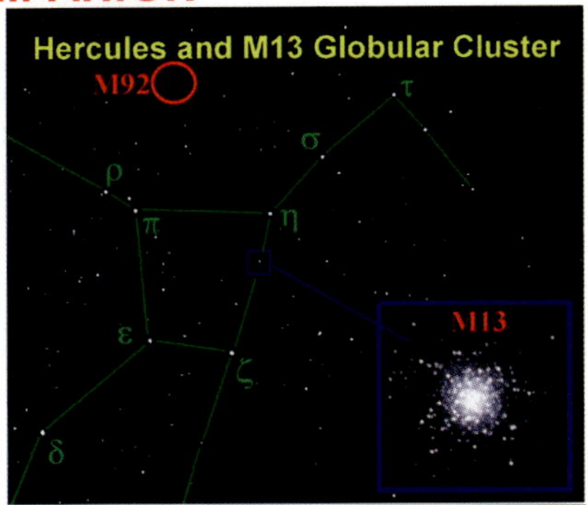

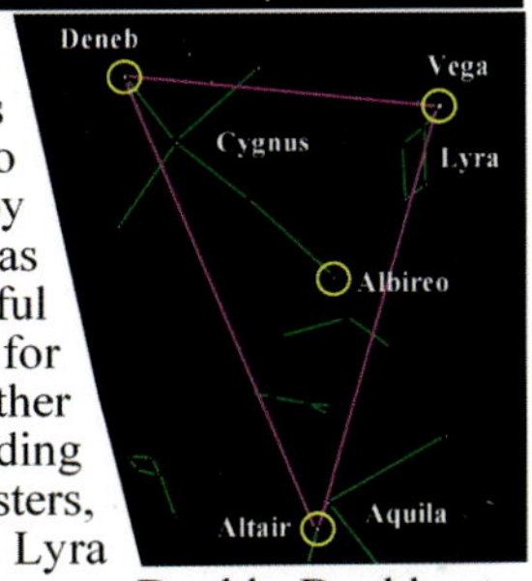

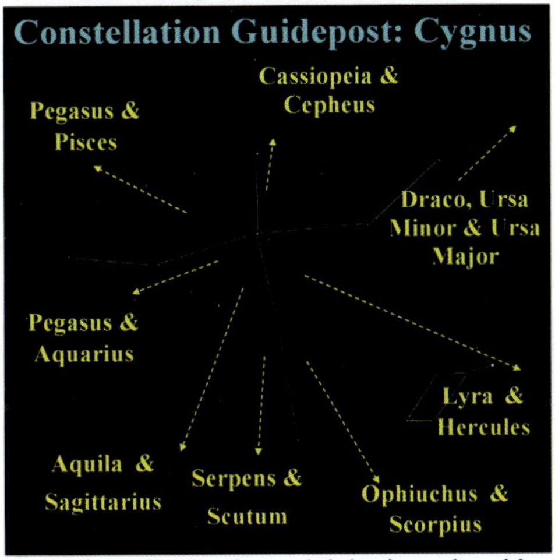

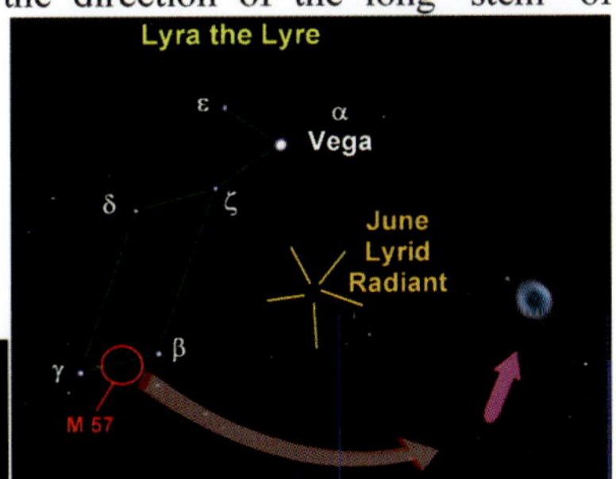

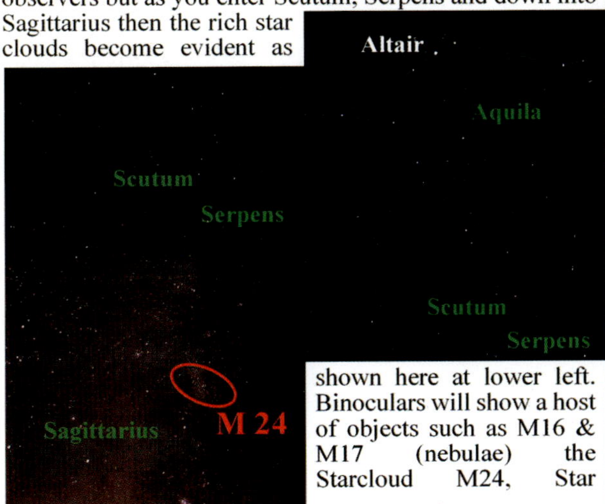

December Night Sky

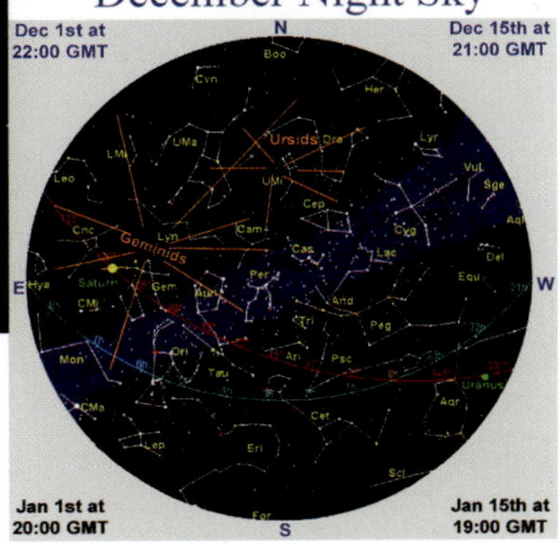

clusters such as M25, M23, M6 and M7 to name just a few. Sagittarius is the Archer although in truth it looks more like a teapot! The Galactic Centre (GC) lies within it not far from the border with neighbouring Scorpius the Scorpion and Ophiuchus the Serpent Bearer. There

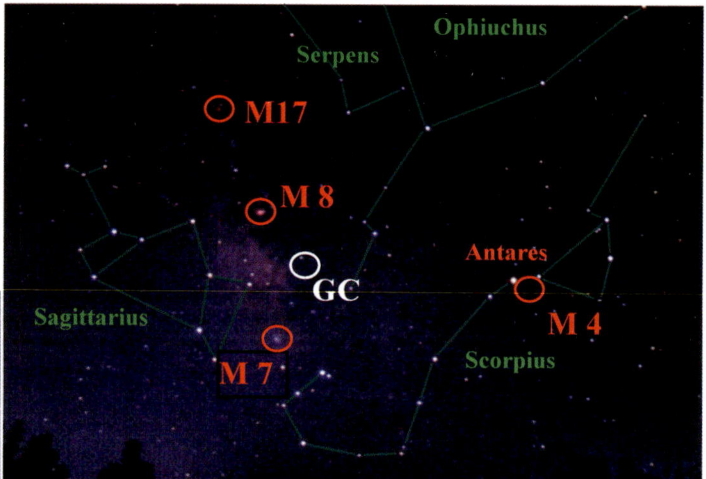

are several star clouds in this region with many globular clusters in particular. Nearby Ophiuchus seems barren in comparison but nonetheless has itself seven Messier objects (all Globulars).

Some of the best objects (but by no means all of them) are shown on this page with M17 a bright Nebula in Serpens, M8 the Lagoon Nebula in Sagittarius, M7 an Open Star Cluster and M4 the wonderful Globular Cluster both in Scorpius. Scorpius is not really seen in all its glory from our Latitudes but travel to somewhere like the Algarve or the Canary Islands and there you can see its tail in all its splendour. Libra the Scales used to be considered the claws of the Scorpion but became a constellation in its own right - although fairly poor for deep sky objects. Scorpius and Sagittarius are both on the Ecliptic but technically so is part of Ophiuchus as well - perhaps there should be thirteen Zodiacal constellations? Moving past Sagittarius we come to Capricornus the Sea Goat which brings us full circle along the Ecliptic. Capricornus is not particularly bright and covers quite a large area but do use binoculars on Alpha Cap as it is a nice wide double whilst there is Messier 30 - a nice Globular Cluster just visible in binoculars There are 88 constellations in the entire sky but not all are visible from our latitudes. In a book of this size it is not possible to cover all that can be seen but it is hoped that the readers appetite has been whetted and there are many books that cover the constellations in more detail.

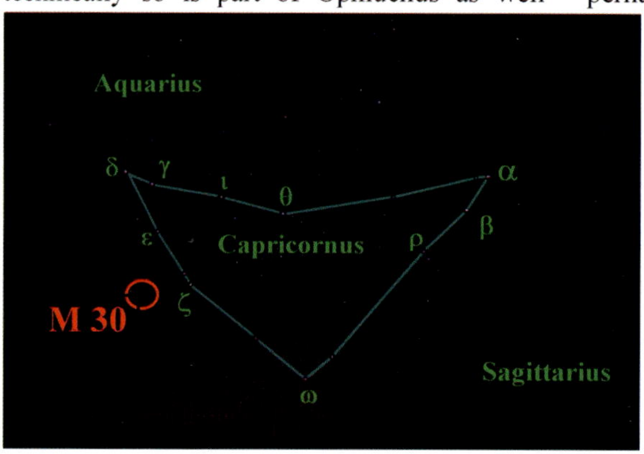